R. C.

John Sutt
2 Cor 4:5-7

W. Robert Godfrey

R C Sproul
Joshua 24:15

Douglas Wilson

Sinclair B. Ferguson

AFTER
DARKNESS,
LIGHT

AFTER DARKNESS, LIGHT

DISTINCTIVES OF REFORMED THEOLOGY

ESSAYS IN HONOR OF
R.C. SPROUL

EDITED BY
R.C. SPROUL JR.

P&R PUBLISHING
P.O. BOX 817 • PHILLIPSBURG • NEW JERSEY 08865-0817

Unless otherwise indicated, Scripture quotations in chapter 1 are from the *NEW AMERICAN STANDARD BIBLE®*. © Copyright The Lockman Foundation 1960, 1962, 1963, 1968, 1971, 1972, 1973, 1975, 1977. Used by permission.

Scripture quotations in chapter 2 are from *The Holy Bible, English Standard Version,* copyright © 2001 by Crossway Bibles, a division of Good News Publishers. Used by permission. All rights reserved.

Scripture quotations in chapters 3 and 6 are from *The Holy Bible, Revised Standard Version,* copyright © 1946, 1952, by the Division of Christian Education of the National Council of the Churches of Christ in the United States of America. All rights reserved.

Unless otherwise indicated, Scripture quotations in chapters 4 and 5 are from the HOLY BIBLE, NEW INTERNATIONAL VERSION®. NIV®. Copyright © 1973, 1978, 1984 by International Bible Society. Used by permission of Zondervan Publishing House. All rights reserved.

Scripture quotations in chapter 7 are taken from the King James Version.

Unless otherwise indicated, Scripture quotations in chapters 8 and 10 are from *The Holy Bible, New King James Version.* Copyright © 1979, 1980, 1982, Thomas Nelson, Inc.

Scripture quotations in chapter 9 are taken from *The Christian Counselor's New Testament.* © 1977 by Jay E. Adams.

Italics within Scripture quotations indicate emphasis added.

Page design by Tobias Design
Typesetting by Michelle Feaster

Printed in the United States of America

Library of Congress Cataloging-in-Publication Data

After darkness, light : distinctives of Reformed theology : essays in honor of R.C. Sproul / edited by R.C. Sproul, Jr.
    p. cm.
   Includes bibliographical references and index.
   ISBN 0-87552-704-3
   1. Calvinism. 2. Reformed Church—Doctrines. I. Sproul, R. C. (Robert Charles), 1939– II. Sproul, R. C. (Robert Craig), 1965–

BX9422.5.A34 2003
230'.42—dc21

2003040493

CONTENTS

FOREWORD

EDMUND P. CLOWNEY

For almost a biblical generation, the ministry of R. C. Sproul has been transforming the convictions of evangelicals. His teaching brought robust Calvinism back into American evangelicalism. He was not alone. Theological education prospered in the same period. Westminster Seminary grew in influence and provided many teachers for Covenant Seminary in St. Louis, for Gordon-Conwell in the Boston area, and for Reformed Seminary in Jackson, Mississippi, and in Orlando, Florida. Other centers for these seminaries have now been established.

For American evangelicalism, R. C. Sproul became a morning star of a new reformation. He organized regional and national conferences and enthralled large audiences of laypeople who attended them. R. C. is a communicator, not a mere lecturer. I once saw him holding an envelope taken from his pocket, on which he had scribbled four or five words. That was the outline for his address. Naturally, he never looked at the envelope when he spoke.

He tells stories, of course, and some became his favorites when he spoke at different places. Yet he was always free to include an observation from an hour or two before. Once he referred to a contemporary situation a bit too casually. Lecturing at Geneva College, he referred to the Latin motto on the college seal: "Christo et patria." Missing the meaning of *patria,* "fatherland," he lamented the absence of the Spirit in the seal. The professor who taught him Latin was in the audience.

Such a story may seem ill-advised in this foreword to a Festschrift in honor of Dr. Sproul. His scholarship is well established and recognized. After majoring in philosophy at Westminster College, he earned a bachelor of divinity degree (now recognized as a master's degree) at Pittsburgh Theological Seminary.

Because he knew of the history of Reformed scholarship in the Netherlands, he went to the Free University of Amsterdam for an extended period of study in theology. He earned the Drs. (*doctorandus*) degree there. Whitefield Theological Seminary recently granted him the Ph.D. degree.

Yet R. C. Sproul has never sought the scholarly recognition that is his due. His learning has always been in the service of the gospel. He has brought Reformed doctrine to people in the pew. His ministry really began when he saw that church members did not understand the Christian faith well enough. John Calvin had defended the position of a "doctor" in the church: a teaching elder given the charge of instructing the people in the doctrines of the Word. Calvin saw that as his own calling. R. C. Sproul, without making any claim to such eminence, has become a "doctor" of the Bible-believing church today.

"Ligonier Ministries" is the label that R. C. uses for his instruction of the laypeople of the church. The name is taken from Ligonier, Pennsylvania, although the center is now based in Orlando, Florida. I recall listening to R. C. in the early seventies, when the center had been established on property in western Pennsylvania given by Mrs. Dora Hillman. His teaching was clear and urgent, and the Lord's gifts blessed his growing ministry. R. C. brought leading Bible teachers to Ligonier. Dr. John Gerstner was one of the first. Francis Schaeffer came; J. I. Packer taught at Ligonier. R. C. is clearly a disciple of John Gerstner, more mellow in manner, but strong in the truth.

From the beginning of Ligonier, Sproul realized the need for spreading his teaching. Ligonier distributed audiotapes, then videotapes in growing numbers. Later he launched radio programs. Above all, he published books dealing with the pressing needs of his large and growing audience. The contributors to this volume show how R. C. Sproul has used the sword of the Spirit to open secular minds to the strong doctrines of Calvinism.

Worship has marked Sproul's ministry increasingly through the years. Surely the doctrines of grace demand adoration of the God who is sovereign in mercy, and who chose in love those who were his enemies. This Festschrift follows the Canons of Dort, which affirm the Reformed doctrine in sharp distinction to Arminianism. The famous five points of Calvinism are all treated here: total depravity, unconditional election, limited (definite) atonement, irresistible grace, and the perseverance of the saints. Sproul himself has always held that declarations should not only make positive affirmations, but also specify what was being denied. As a member of the International Council on Biblical Inerrancy, he took the lead in forging denials that drove to the heart of the matter. His convictions on the *"solas,"* also treated in this book, also sharpen the distinctions that make the truth clear. God's grace alone justifies, not his grace plus our works.

Yet for all his zeal to distinguish and define, R. C. worships before the mystery of God's salvation. The apostle Paul broke into heavenly doxologies to rejoice in the infinite wisdom and goodness of the Lord. Yet Paul knew well that human eloquence never brings God's wisdom to earth. His foolishness shames the wise. He sweeps aside human eloquence with the foolishness of the gospel. "The foolishness of God is wiser than men, and the weakness of God is stronger than men." Mysteries before which archangels fall silent Paul stated in the brief words, "I determined to know nothing among you except Jesus Christ and him crucified."

R. C. Sproul has, in his tapes and writings, argued each of the points covered in the chapters of this book, yet he has done so with the example of the apostle Paul before him. Simple directness shines through all his preaching and writing. This book is dedicated to R. C. Sproul in appreciation of one who sought to build the faith of Christ's church, that it might rest not in the wisdom of men, but in the power of God.

INTRODUCTION

R. C. SPROUL JR.

It was a hero of mine who first warned me that heroes have feet of clay. This put me in something of a pickle. If my hero had no feet of clay, then he at least had these feet of clay, that he was unduly pessimistic about heroes. If, on the other hand, my hero spoke with wisdom on the matter, then he too had feet of clay. I solved the dilemma by adding to the admirable qualities of my hero that he was humble and had an appropriate level of skepticism about lesser mortals than he.

It is a natural thing for a young boy to look up to his father, to see him as a hero. It was all the more natural for me, as I grew up understanding that there were many others who saw my father as their hero. But it was all the more natural for me, for in my circumstance the term fit. He may have been my father, but my assessment of him was true.

Why my father was and is my hero has changed over the years. When I was a small boy, it was enough that he loved me and my sister and my mother. It was enough that he knew how to fix my kite, or that he took me with him to the golf course. It was still greater that he took me more than once. The first time he took me, I was five. He took two practice swings on the first tee. As he began his downswing, I called out from the cart, "One more strike and you're out, Daddy." Luckily for me, he only fouled that one off.

As I grew, my father grew in my estimation. About the time that my sights went beyond his tenderness to me, I came across a treasure chest. I was about eight years old and was rooting around in the cellar of our home. I found there an old steamer trunk and opened it up. What I found was a veritable reliquary, overflowing with icons of my father's past greatness. There was a newspaper photo of him driving a double down the left field line in a high school baseball game. There was a varsity letter from Thomas Jefferson Junior High School, and another from Clairton High, both in Pittsburgh. There was also a baseball, signed not by the Pittsburgh Pirates of yore, but by his grateful teammates, after he had carried them on his shoulders to victory. That treasure, I am sorry to report, got lost one day when, owing to the loss of all my own baseballs, its sentimental value to me was outweighed by its practical value in allowing the game to continue. Soon after, it joined the other balls in that netherworld of lost balls.

Now in my mind's eye, my father joined those newer heroes who were beginning to try to crowd him out. He told me stories about his baseball career, about how he had been invited to try out for a place in the Pirates' farm system, but passed on such a long shot. (There was that cursed pessimism of his.) He told me of his exploits on the football field, how in high school he had served as the backup for Ron Lancaster, who went on to become the Johnny Unitas of the Canadian Football League. My father became then not unlike Terry Bradshaw and Willie Stargell to me. He also told stories of his basketball career, and his exploits in hockey and boxing.

But the two most significant events in my father's life derailed any thoughts of future glory on the fields of play. The first was the death of his hero, his father. My grandfather was the second of the Sproul men to be named Robert C. He owned a thriving accounting firm in downtown Pittsburgh. He provided well for his family, but also served as a model of godliness for my father. Although his age would have precluded his being drafted, he volunteered for the war in the aftermath of Pearl Harbor, and served his country by working with the quartermasters in the European theater. During the war and after, the Sproul home became a sort of haven as uncles, aunts, and cousins lived under my grandfather's roof, along with my father, his sister, and his mother. The war ended and brought my grandfather safely home.

As my father passed into adolescence, however, his father's health began to fail. A series of strokes left him debilitated. The need to help care for him, and to help provide for the family, forced my father to give up his array of sports. Finally, when my father was seventeen, his father spoke his last words: "I have fought the good fight, I have finished the race, I have kept the faith." At seventeen, my father buried his hero.

His exploits in sports earned my father a scholarship to Westminster College, a small Presbyterian school in western Pennsylvania. Here too, however, he never got a chance to shine. Before his freshman season had even begun, while trying to catch a wayward tomato that had fallen from his tray in the cafeteria, he damaged a knee sufficiently to rule out competitive sports.

The second life-changing event came soon thereafter. My father was in the common area of a dorm at school when one of the older players on the football team began a conversation. Beginning with the fact that a life under the sun promises only futility, this young man presented the unvarnished gospel of the Son. That night, there was no close, no praying of the sinner's prayer. Instead, my father retired to his room to wrestle with the angel of the Lord. He knew that he could make no half-hearted commitment. He understood that if he picked up this cross, if he followed this Jesus, it would mean his whole life. Finally, the Spirit of God, like the pale Galilean, conquered, and my father repented, believed the gospel, and professed that Christ is Lord.

Only two critical parts of the story remain before my arrival on the scene. First, my father spoke with my mother about what had happened. She was a sophomore at Wooster College in Ohio. She had known my father since the two of them had been in grade school. They had been steadies off and on, mostly on, all through high school. At first she was puzzled by this change in my father, but my mother was soon likewise convicted of her sin, of her need for the Savior, and of the work of Christ on her behalf. Now the two of them were bound together in Christ.

The rest of the early part of the story is my father's education. After his conversion, he nearly flunked out of college. His time was consumed with reading the Bible and with studying the sermons of Billy Graham. That didn't leave much time for other disciplines. But then my father attended a lecture on the philosophy of Augustine. When the lecture ended, he headed for the registrar's office to change majors. The same professor not only introduced my father to the study of philosophy, but also to the doctrines of grace. Like so many before him and so many since, my father struggled mightily against the sovereignty of God. By God's grace, God won.

My parents were married the summer before my father's senior year at Westminster College. After graduating, he enrolled at Pittsburgh Theological Seminary, a seminary of what was then the United Presbyterian Church. Like so many other seminaries in that day and today, this one was dominated by unbelief. The faculty could be counted on to deny the inerrancy of Scripture, the virgin birth, the resurrection of Christ, and anything else that might prove inconvenient to the spirit of the age. However, the faculty was not monolithic. The seminary had been formed by the merger of two older seminaries. The smaller of the two, the more conservative seminary, managed in their negotiations to secure a spot on the faculty for their young theological hero, John Gerstner.

Dr. Gerstner believed that the Bible was true and that it taught with clarity what we know as the Reformed faith. He taught that faith with vigor and with logical and theological precision to my father. And my father became a zealot for the Reformed faith. As graduation from seminary approached, my parents, now toting about my older sister, Sherrie, looked forward to the end of schooling and to getting on with their life's work. Dr. Gerstner insisted that my father pursue further study. His advice was to study with the best, and that meant G. C. Berkouwer at the Free University of Amsterdam. My parents sold what little they owned and sailed with my sister to the Netherlands.

My own recollection of those days is rather sketchy, as I experienced them in utero. But in my father's fictional novel,

Thy Brother's Keeper, there is a tale about a young American theology student in Amsterdam, who is forced to spend many hours learning the Dutch language by reading Dutch works of theology, writing down each word and its translation, one word at a time. My father distinguished himself as a student and even was written up in the local paper because of his prowess on the baseball field.

An opportunity to teach at his alma mater brought him home to America. This brief stint was followed by teaching at colleges and seminaries in Boston and Philadelphia, and finally a position as associate minister of theology at a large United Presbyterian Church in Cincinnati. This covered roughly the years from 1965 to 1971. While teaching in academia and in the church, he also had opportunities to teach at camps and conferences. It was at Saranac Lake in New York that he first taught on the holiness of God.

Back in Pittsburgh, he was not forgotten. A group of men dreamed of opening a study center that would serve as a kind of battlefield seminary for laypersons who were actively engaged in ministry. They asked my father if he would be the principal teacher there and run this ministry. He accepted the call, and our family moved to the Ligonier Valley in western Pennsylvania.

During the early 1970s, the nation was reeling from hardships abroad and at home. American involvement in the Vietnam War was drawing to a close. The sexual revolution had just hit its stride. The president was virtually forced to resign his office. The age of Aquarius was disintegrating as young people looked for something more substantial than "tune in, turn on, and drop out." Many of those seekers found their way to the nascent Ligonier Valley Study Center. There they found not only shelter from the storm, but teaching that was at the same time biblical, theological, and practical. They were taught the Reformed faith, in all its fullness.

The study center grew slowly. Although I was sheltered from such things, I have been told that there were many months when there were no paychecks. But the study center was founded on a call to faithfulness, not on a carefully laid out business plan. In time, God began to reward that faithfulness as the ministry grew. In 1975, in what may have been the first use of videotape technology in Christian education, my father filmed his first version of *The Holiness of God*. Ligonier not only had to persuade people of the value of the teaching, but often had to train churches to use video.

Over the years, the study center gradually shifted its emphasis. It began training young men and women involved in campus ministry. Before long, my father became involved with an organization called Value of the Person, a Christian management-consulting ministry that emphasized something as simple and biblical as the importance of treating employees with dignity. My father spoke on this theme in boardrooms and steel mills. Eventually the study center provided training for hundreds in management at a nearby Volkswagon plant.

The study center hosted a summit meeting among evangelicals committed to the inerrancy of the Bible. Out of those meetings came the Ligonier Statement on the Inerrancy of the Bible. My father also served on the board of the International Council on Biblical Inerrancy, and for a time as its president.

There was also a strategic partnership with Prison Fellowship. Now our students were neither businessmen nor parachurch ministry workers, but prisoners who were allowed out on furlough to be trained in teaching the Bible inside prison. The variety of students, however, did not cause a diffusion of purpose, as Ligonier and my father continued to impress on people the biblical truths of the Reformation.

In 1977, the first issue of *Tabletalk* magazine was issued as a tool to keep our constituents apprised of the events at the study center. Today my father's monthly column, "Right Now Counts Forever," reaches over seventy thousand subscribers in the United States and around the world. My father's ministry, both at Ligonier and around the world, continued to grow, as audiotapes and videotapes went out to students who could not make it to the study center, and as he continued to publish more books.

In 1982, my father's first radio program, "The R. C. Sproul Study Hour," went on the air. Out of that grew verse-by-verse expositions of several books of the Bible that were later published in book form, and which for several years served as the substance of the daily studies in *Tabletalk*.

At the same time, my father was becoming more and more sought after as a conference speaker. Tape sales continued to grow, and the Ligonier Board of Directors decided that it was no longer sound stewardship to invest our donors' funds in the upkeep of the study center campus. So in 1984 the Ligonier Valley Study Center became Ligonier Ministries and moved to Orlando, Florida. By God's grace, the outreach of Ligonier grew faster than it ever had before.

In the last fifteen years or so, my father has taught at several different seminaries, written dozens of books, grown the *Renewing Your Mind* radio program to the point that it is now heard on over three hundred radio stations around the world, and now serves as senior minister of preaching at Saint Andrews Chapel. He has continued, like his father before him, to fight the good fight. He has continued, with single-minded purpose, to teach people the holiness and sovereignty of our God.

God has gifted my father with a powerful mix of gifts. He is committed to the Reformed faith. He is passionate without being strident. He has a zeal for teaching the laity. And he is a gifted communicator. Like few scholars before him, my father has the ability to take what can at times seem to be complicated theological issues and make them understandable for the nonprofessional. He is able to simplify, without becoming simplistic. These gifts he has returned to the King, that they might be of service in the building of his kingdom.

His public ministry began to grow with the publication of his first book, *The Symbol.* This book, first published by Presbyterian and Reformed in 1973, was designed to help laypeople understand the historic faith as it is laid out in the Apostles' Creed. It is on the occasion of the thirtieth anniversary of the release of this book that we are honoring my father for his work and ministry.

The contributors to this book reflect two different elements of my father's ministry. Over the years, he has worked side by side with other great men of the faith. With some he served on the International Council on Biblical Inerrancy. With others he has fought battles over Evangelicals and Catholics Together. With still others he has labored to keep the work of Bible translation free of the yeast of "political correctness." Many of these colaborers have been gracious enough to contribute to this work. Many of them have described this opportunity to honor my father as an honor to them. But my father has always been, first and last, a teacher. So other contributors are former students of my father's, each now about the business of teaching others about the doctrines of grace. These are men who began as his students, and, because of his faithful teaching, have come to be colaborers.

There are, sadly, two important names missing from our

list of contributors—two men who, if they were still with us, would have been delighted to be listed. James Montgomery Boice was always a friend to my father and a fellow soldier. Each encouraged the other. As long as they both labored, neither could cry out, like Elijah, "I alone am left, O Lord." We regret that his untimely death kept him from these pages. John Gerstner was to my father first a teacher and finally a co-laborer. But throughout his life, Dr. Gerstner was a hero to my hero. He modeled both the theological precision and the zeal that have marked my father's work from the beginning. He was a man who feared no man, but feared God. He was a man whose personal holiness outshone his theological acumen. Both Dr. Boice and Dr. Gerstner spent their lives teaching and defending the sovereign grace of God, and now they enjoy the fullest communion with our common Lord. Both men likewise commune with the souls of just men made perfect. And both men, from the vantage point of the throne of the Lamb, would echo the sentiments of our only true Hero, "Well done, thou good and faithful servant."

Our goal in this work is actually two goals that fold into one. We do want to honor my father for his faithful labors over the years. We enjoy a long tradition of works written to honor scholars for their life's work. (In fact, my father edited *Soli Deo Gloria,* a Festschrift in honor of John Gerstner on the occasion of his retirement from Pittsburgh Theological Seminary.) The sad truth, however, is that too many of these works become hollow trophies. They languish as unread historical markers. My father, however, has always believed that theology belongs to everyone. He has made it the center of his life's work, like that thundering bull Martin Luther, to teach the laity the fullness of the holiness of God, which finds its expression in the Reformed faith.

10

We honor my father, then, by creating a book for everyone. What you hold is not a dusty, erudite tome, but a heartfelt celebration of the doctrines that define the Reformed faith and so define my father's ministry. Our hope is that thousands who read this book will not only conclude that my father is a great man, but, more importantly, that he serves a great and sovereign God. Our goal is not that the ranks of those who see my father as a hero will swell, but rather that our vision of our true Hero will swell. Our goal, like Calvin's, is that as we understand the doctrines of grace better, we will worship God better.

As much, however, as people look to my father as a hero, they do not and cannot love him as I do. He was first a hero to me because he was my father. He was next a hero to me because of his prowess in sports. As I grew older, he became a hero to me because he was a soldier for the Reformed faith. But now, once again, as I seek to raise up warriors for the kingdom of God in my own children, he is a hero because he is my father. His work continues as I seek to raise his grandchildren in the nurture and admonition of the Lord, despite my own feet of clay. Together, all we who have been bought by the blood of the Son labor to make manifest the reign of that Son over all things.

Though man knows not his time, we do know that our days are few. That is not cause for despair. Instead, it should be a goad for us, that we would give our lives in useful service. And it should be a joy to us who are in Christ Jesus, for we know that we will soon be like him, for we shall see him as he is. When that day comes for my father, I pray that the last words he will hear from his son are the last words he heard from his father, "You have fought the good fight, you have finished the race, you have kept the faith." And then he will be ushered in to receive a crown of righteousness.

1

TOTAL DEPRAVITY

MARTIN MURPHY

The seminary professor took his usual position to begin his lecture, but on this occasion he looked rather seriously at the students and said, "Man is very, very bad and God is very, very mad." Professor Sproul then proceeded with his lecture on total depravity. Widely spoken of, but barely believed in today, total depravity holds a prominent place in the history of the Protestant church. To recover the doctrine is necessary for the good health of the church.

Total depravity explains the biblical doctrine of sin. It brings the nature of man to the forefront of our consciousness. Is his nature good or evil? Does he sin because he is a sinner or because of the sin in his environment? Theologians and philosophers try to explain sin in terms of moral responsibilities. Since moral responsibilities have no objective standard in postmodern relativism, a definitive statement of the doctrine of sin is necessary. Sin refers to any disposition or action that does not measure up to God's perfect standard of righteousness. Jonathan Edwards said, "Sin is self-love without God." The redefinition of sin in the postmodern world seems to exclude everything except abuse of the environment. Today sin is merely the bad example of good people.

THE ROOTS OF TULIP

The acronym known as TULIP, representing what are often called "the five points of Calvinism," summarizes the doctrine of God's sovereign grace. Total depravity is the first of the five points, but the doctrine did not originate with John Calvin. He did attempt to recover the biblical doctrine, which has a long history. The doctrine became a major area of debate during the seventeenth century. The root of the controversy can be traced to the teaching of the Dutch theologian Jacobus Arminius (Jakob Hermandszoon). His followers remonstrated (protested) against the Calvinistic or Reformed system of doctrine. The controversy was settled at the Synod of Dort (1618–19), held in the Netherlands, which condemned the Arminian doctrine and removed the Remonstrants from their pulpits. In their third and fourth main points, the Synod rejected the Arminian teaching "that unregenerate man is not strictly or totally dead in his sins or deprived of all capacity for spiritual good but is able to hunger and thirst for righteousness of life and to offer the sacrifice of a broken and contrite spirit which is pleasing to God." Despite the Synod of Dort, Arminianism did not die out; it remained a popular doctrine. For instance, the system of doctrine developed by John Wesley was Arminian, and in fact his movement was known as "Arminianism on fire." There has been a large spillover of certain tenets of Arminianism into most evangelical churches, and it remains widespread today.

What do Arminians believe? In the seventeenth century, an assessment would have been relatively simple to make, but in the twentieth century the divisions within Arminianism are multiple. Millard Erickson, an evangelical theologian, gives this definition:

> Arminianism holds that God's decision to give salvation to certain persons and not to others is based upon his fore-knowledge of who will believe. It also includes the idea that genuinely regenerated [born again] people can lose their salvation. . . . Arminianism often has a less serious view of human depravity than does Calvinism.[1]

Arminians do not take human depravity seriously enough because they do not take the righteousness of God seriously enough.

THE STANDARD: GOD'S RIGHTEOUSNESS

To understand the concept of human depravity, we must consider God's righteousness in contrast to man's unrighteousness. The Bible teaches the righteousness of God. God is just. He created righteous Adam, but Adam was not content to be a sinless, rational creature, so he believed Satan's lie and became a fool. Adam worshiped an idol, rather than the Creator. As a result, man is now a sinner. God made a covenant with Adam, and Adam broke it. Breaking that covenant provoked the wrath of God.

The doctrine of the wrath of God is detestable, according to many people. Instead, the love of God is the centerpiece of our day. The love of God is important, to be sure, but God's love can never be seen until sinners see the wrath of God. If God is righteous, then he must pour out his wrath on the human race (Gen. 2:15; 3:1ff.). The righteousness of God is evident from his judgment and wrath. The people of God in the Old Testament, from the time of Moses to the destruction of the temple in 586 B.C., provoked the Lord to wrath (Deut. 9:7; 2 Chron. 28:25; Ezek. 8:17). God's wrath is his righteous response to evil. The wrath of God in the New Testament is expressed in different ways. For instance, the wrath of God is mentioned in the gospel of John: "He who believes in the Son has eternal life; but he who does not obey the Son shall not see life, but the wrath of God abides on him" (John 3:36). From this passage you can see that the wrath of God is not an emotional outburst of anger. It is simply the punishment due for disobedience to God. The little phrase "the wrath of God" comes from the Greek words *orgē theou*. It was a common expression used by ancient cultures. When people experienced a storm, earthquake, volcano, flood, or even an enemy invasion, they would cry out, "The wrath of god(s)!" They thought they were being punished by their gods for the misbehavior of the people.

We must distinguish between the wrath of God and the wrath of man. God's wrath is sinless. It is his punitive justice. "Therefore thus says the Lord GOD, 'Behold, My anger and My wrath will be poured out on this place, on man and on beast and on the trees of the field and on the fruit of the ground; and it will burn and not be quenched'" (Jer. 7:20). The sin of idolatry and disobedience continued to provoke God's anger (Judg. 2:11–15).

Man's wrath comes from a sinful creature and is often an expression of cruelty, injustice, and oppression. Man's wrath is a restless and uncontrollable passion. The object of God's wrath is the unrighteous man. Unrighteousness is a universal condition of the human race. The first evidence of unrighteousness is idolatry. Idolatry leads to immoral behavior, social evils, and, when taken to its logical end, pure anarchy. The inspired apostle Paul asserts that "the wrath of God is revealed from heaven against all ungodliness and unrighteousness of men, who suppress the truth in unrighteousness" (Rom. 1:18). The end of idolatry is a debased mind. It is not a matter of God's anger demonstrated against men. It is God's wrath demonstrated against the ungodliness and unrighteousness of men. God's wrath is poured out upon unrighteous men because of his justice.

The revelation of God's wrath is natural to all men. To put it another way, God's wrath is a general revelation. It is a universal principle. Both God's righteousness and his wrath are known to the minds of men because God has made them known (Rom. 1:18–19). Since God does not withhold his wrath, universal sinfulness is a fundamental biblical doctrine (Rom. 1:18–3:23). The relationship between human beings and God is not one of good men and a kinder, gentler God. Total depravity not only encompassed Adam; it extends to his descendants.

CORRUPTION OF MAN'S WHOLE NATURE

The doctrine of original sin is one aspect of total depravity. The biblical doctrine of original sin refers to the place and effect of Adam's first sin. The place is the human heart. The

17

effect is the whole nature of man in body and soul. The human mind, will, and affections are corrupt. John Calvin asserts that original sin is "a hereditary depravity and corruption of our nature, diffused into all parts of the soul, which first makes us liable to God's wrath."[2] Pelagius, a monk who lived more than 1500 years ago, denied the doctrine of total depravity by rejecting the biblical doctrine of original sin. Pelagius believed that Adam's sin affected Adam, but not the entire human race. Therefore, he rejected the biblical doctrine that newborn infants are sinners when they come into the world.

Contrary to the teaching of Pelagius, the Bible teaches that the effect of sin is universal. Original sin is the source of all actual sins. The Westminster divines described original sin as "original corruption, whereby we are utterly indisposed, disabled, and made opposite to all good, and wholly inclined to all evil."[3] Calvin and Westminster have given a biblical argument for the innate dimension of original sin. Man is totally corrupt in all his faculties of body and soul.

A CORRUPT MIND

Since one of the faculties of the soul is the mind, any consideration of total depravity must include the mind. The mind is the source of all rational thought. It is the seat of intelligence. Theologians sometimes refer to the noetic effect of the Fall to describe the depraved mind. The terms are useful because *noetic* comes from the Greek word *nous,* translated "mind" in the New Testament. God gave Adam and his descendants intellect. The reasoning processes of human beings set them apart from all other creatures. The Fall did not destroy the intellect or the reasoning processes, but it did cause the intellect to function irrationally. Total depravity does not mean that

18

man's mental faculties were destroyed by sin. It does mean that they were disabled, defiled, and injured by sin. Before the Fall, Adam could not make a mathematical mistake or engage in any faulty reasoning. After the Fall, he and all of his progeny became faulty in their intellect and reasoning processes. To put it another way, the mind is subject to misunderstanding truth. The noetic effect of sin leaves the mind in a state of confusion. The Bible says that depraved minds "did not like to retain God in their knowledge" (Rom. 1:28 NKJV). Therefore, the depraved mind has no pleasure in the knowledge of God.

The natural state of man after the Fall is to bear the guilt of Adam's sin, not his sin itself. Guilt implies punishment. The desire of all humanity is to repress the knowledge of God, since that knowledge is the haunting punishment for the sin of idolatry. Men cannot think about the nature and character of God because they are reminded of the punishment that will come from his hand. Human beings cope with the prospect of punishment by pursuing diversions. These diversions are the only relief available for the totally depraved mind.

The insanity of the godless mind is apparent in every area of life. Family life has become a utilitarian arrangement rather than a God-appointed institution under his law. Educational institutions reflect an anti-intellectual disposition. The judicial system is a house of indiscriminate subjectivity, rather than a place of objective justice. The political system is a safe harbor for depravity.

A CORRUPT WILL

The opponents of the doctrine of total depravity teach that sin is a moral habit or a psychological illness. The cure for sin, they say, is character reformation. The instruction given to the patient may be a three-step program or a ten-step program.

But it doesn't matter how many steps one takes; the recovery program is futile. The Fall left the will unable to perform any spiritual good. The will is the part of the soul that makes decisions or choices according to its inclination. Total inability is the appropriate designation for the fallen will. Before the Fall, every decision was in perfect harmony with the intellect. Every decision was in perfect harmony with God's law. After the Fall, the will has been unable to choose any spiritual good. The Fall rendered the human will a "slave to sin." Although fallen man may perform an outward act of moral good, his motive is evil. Motivation is the consciousness of a desire for an object. Motive is the principle upon which people make choices. There is a motive for every decision. William Graham explains that "the appetite and desires embrace all the objects in nature and each suggests its particular object and craves for indulgence, and although some of them subside, others do not and whilst either of these is in action, we are not without desire and consequently not without a motive to solicit our choice."[4] The object of fallen man's gratification is his own ego. The prophet Isaiah addressed self-gratification relative to the exaltation of the depraved ego. Although God used Babylon to punish Israel, Babylon boasted that "I am, and there is no one besides me" (Isa. 47:8). Since fallen man's object is his own ego, he will choose self-deification.

In such passages as Colossians 2:13, the Bible teaches that "you who were dead in trespasses . . . God made alive." Man is *not able* to change his motives. The inheritance of the guilt of sin is the basis of man's moral inability to choose that which is pleasing to God. The "hearts of the sons of men are full of evil" (Eccl. 9:3). The prophet Jeremiah said, "The heart is deceitful above all things, and desperately corrupt" (Jer. 17:9 RSV). All men are born in sin, and their will is to do the desire of their father, the devil (John 8:44). In fact, "there is not a righteous man on earth who continually does good and who never sins" (Eccl. 7:20). Man is so helpless in the matter of eternal salvation that God has to give him faith in order for him to believe (Eph. 2:1–10).

The ideas, concepts, and principles behind the doctrine of total inability sometimes seem abstract and incommunicable. But the Lord left us with an agricultural metaphor to help us understand the doctrine. He said, "You will know them by their fruits. Do men gather grapes from thornbushes or figs from thistles? Even so, every good tree bears good fruit, but a bad tree bears bad fruit" (Matt. 7:16–17 NKJV). Grapes are good and tasty to the appetite. Thorns are a nuisance and inedible. Figs contain vital nutrients. Thistles are useless. These two types of plants represent the outward evidences of inward conditions. One represents the useless and depraved nature. The other represents a healthy and restored nature. The nature of the plant produces the fruit. The human will after the Fall is a slave to sin and unable to do any spiritual good.

CORRUPT AFFECTIONS

The intellect and the will find expression in that faculty of the soul known as the affections. This part of the soul is also called the emotions. As a function of the soul, the emotions express the moral judgments of the sinful mind and the motive of the will. Personal preferences may or may not fall into the category of moral judgments. Does that mean that some preferences are expressions of sin and others are not? Every day we make decisions that fall into the category of *adiaphora*. This Greek term means "things indifferent." For instance, if you decide to paint your room green rather than blue, it may be a matter of *adiaphora*. It is not a sin to use blue paint. However, if the blue paint costs twice as much as the green paint, then the moral judgment is whether or not you are being a good steward of God's resources. After consideration of the preference, the emotional response may be apprehension before the painting or anger after the painting. Anger may not be sinful, because Jesus is said to have been angry. The Bible commands Christians to "be angry, and do not sin" (Eph. 4:26 NKJV). The expressions of judgments and preferences are sorrow, fear, grief, compassion, sadness, love, and apprehension, to mention a few. The corrupt nature of the emotions causes a man to hate when he should love, or to express joy when he should mourn, and so forth.

DEPRAVITY AND SANCTIFICATION

The doctrine of total depravity explains that the inheritance of the defaced image was more than a demotion from the affluent upper class to the lower middle class. Depravity negatively affects the sinner's relationship with God and his relationship with other people. The Fall causes man to see himself differently than how God sees him. God's system of justice requires absolute sinlessness. God declares his elect righteous in the heavenly courts. His grace solves the problem, but is the converted sinner still totally depraved in his mind, will, and emotions? The answer is yes. Then you ask, "If God declares the Christian righteous, then why is he still a sinner?" A proper understanding of the doctrine of sanctification explains how a converted soul remains totally depraved.

The Reformers' explanation is that the believer is *simul justus et peccator*—"at once righteous and a sinner." The Westminster divines were correct to say that Christians are "renewed in the whole man after the image of God,"[5] but they would also recognize, as G. C. Berkouwer has, that Christian warfare is inseparably connected with the sinful nature.

Sanctification is not an event that is singular and passive on the part of the believer. Christians are expected to produce the fruit of the faith in their own lives. The Christian life consists of growing in personal holiness, which is often described in the Bible as a walk, and walking takes action. The complement to God's sovereign grace is man's pursuit of personal holiness. God has always expected cleansing as a part of his relationship with his people.

Ethical standards must reflect the holiness of God. God's standard is perfection. "Therefore you are to be perfect, as your heavenly Father is perfect" (Matt. 5:48). The standard is so high that Christians often confuse virtue, ethics, and holiness. The word *virtue* in biblical usage refers to moral goodness. Biblical ethics prescribe moral obligations. In his work on moral philosophy, Alasdair MacIntyre argues that modernity should return to an Aristotelian ethic.[6] But MacIntyre, who claims to be a Christian, has confused holiness with a system of subjective ethics. God's holiness is beyond the measure of an ethical system in a sinful world. The holiness of God is perfect and without any need for transformation. The depraved believer does not perfect holiness. While the believer remains depraved throughout life, his character and conduct continue to be transformed by the sanctifying power of the Holy Spirit.

The early Reformers saw the depth of the depravity of converted sinners and realized that they could never be entirely or completely without sin and therefore could never experience entire sanctification. John Calvin said:

In urging men to perfection we must not toil slowly or list-
lessly, much less give up. However I say it is a devilish in-
vention for our minds, while as yet we are in the earthly
race, to be cocksure about our perfection.[7]

Romans 6 teaches the principles of sanctification that are
appropriate for Christians. The apostle Paul contrasts the ten-
sions that characterize all Christians. For example, sin may
seem to prevail in our body, but it will not destroy our soul.
Sin will affect the whole being of the Christian, and yet the
Christian is not a slave to sin. Romans 6 reminds us of the
Christian position in Christ and what one can expect from being in that position. The apostle is not debating the ethical dimensions of the Christian life. As James Montgomery Boice
explains, "The New Testament does not tell us to be what we
will become. Rather, it tells us to be what we are."[8] Romans 6
is speaking in a forensic or legal sense, not an experiential
sense. The doctrine of Romans 6 must find its way into our
lives. The apostle Paul speaks about the Christian experience
in Romans 7, and to that I now turn.

In Romans 7, Paul describes the real life of the Christian.
In the early part of the chapter, he illustrates and explicates the
Old Testament law. He explains how the Christian may know
the clear distinctions between right and wrong. The apostle
goes on to show that the law provokes sin, and then Romans
7:14–25 explains the great battle that occurs within the Christian. Paul describes the inner struggle that takes place in the
life of the Christian.

An age-old controversy surrounds Romans 7:14–25. The
great argument is whether or not this passage is talking about
a believer or an unbeliever. Arminian doctrine leans toward
this passage speaking about the unbeliever, and Calvinistic

doctrine leans toward it speaking about the believer. Paul says things like:

I am of flesh. (v. 14)

That which I am doing, I do not understand. (v. 15)

I do the very thing I do not wish to do. (v. 16)

I know that nothing good dwells in me. (v. 18)

I practice the very evil that I do not wish. (v. 19)

I am doing the very thing I do not wish. (v. 20)

Wretched man that I am! (v. 24)

Any Christian who would read this chapter should not be shocked to find the great apostle Paul talking like this. Paul understood both the character of God and his own character, and realized what a tremendous chasm separated the two. He understood the depth of the depravity of his soul.

The apostle Paul elsewhere discusses the concept of "babes in Christ" (1 Cor. 3:1–2). A "babe" will not have much self-control. Paul has already discussed the fact that Christians are still influenced by the Evil One. So we find in Romans 7:14–25 the story of a "babe" (Christian) who has become aware of sin and hates it, but has not developed sufficiently to digest red meat. This is further evidence of the depraved Christian struggling along the road of sanctification, but nonetheless making progress.

The expressions used in Romans 7:14–25 indicate a deep

sense of personal experience. When we examine our life in the light of God's law, we realize like the apostle Paul that we always fall short of the good that is required of us; thus we find total depravity. The perfectionist says that Paul is not speaking of himself in this passage, but rather is speaking of his formerly unregenerate state. This is rather illogical, because it would follow that once Paul came to faith in Jesus Christ, he never again struggled with sin. That would be nice, but it just does not work out that way in our Christian experience. Paul gives us this passage to comfort us in our walk with the Lord.

Does this mean that we have a license to sin? "May it never be!" (Rom. 6:2). Yet the more we grow in sanctification, the more we understand of the depth of our sin, and so the more wretched we seem to be. But we will be victorious in the end: "The Spirit Himself bears witness with our spirit that we are children of God, and if children, heirs also, heirs of God and fellow-heirs with Christ, if indeed we suffer with Him in order that we may also be glorified with Him" (Rom. 8:16–17). The Christian will suffer from the pains of sin throughout life, but in the final analysis he will be glorified with Christ Jesus. The process of sanctification is a victory. It is a victory because Christians live in the Spirit. A struggle is not an indication of defeat. The flesh and the Spirit are two opposing elements, but the flesh is diminishing and the Spirit is increasing.

ABSOLUTE DEPRAVITY?

Total depravity must be taken seriously, but it must not be mistaken for absolute depravity. Absolute depravity refers to the soul being as bad as it could possibly be. Unconverted, totally depraved people "show the work of the Law written in their hearts" (Rom. 2:15). When the natural man makes a decision to act a certain way, that action reflects his morality. For instance, when an unbeliever becomes angry with another person, what restrains the unbeliever from murder? He does not feel constrained by the law of God contained in the Word of God, yet he does not murder. Why do many unbelievers not commit adultery, steal, or bear false witness? How does the unbeliever keep the law of God, if he does not know the law of God? The answer must be that the law of God is implanted in the hearts of men. The law of God was naturally implanted in the heart of Adam and all his progeny. God put his law in the human heart long before he put it on tablets of stone. If the law of God was natural to Adam and his progeny, where did natural law come from? It came from God. Man is dependent for his morality on the Independent Being who created him. It would be out of character for that Independent Being to allow the dependent being to self-destruct, which would be the logical end for absolute depravity. The Bible asserts and experience affirms that some unregenerate sinners are far worse than others, but they are not absolutely depraved.

A CALL FOR THEOLOGICAL INTEGRITY

Holy Scripture indubitably teaches the fall of the human race into a state of sin and misery. Calvinism takes the doctrine of the Fall very seriously. The Bible declares that man is totally ruined in body and soul. Man is unable to save himself from guilt and condemnation. So then why do most evangelical Christians preach and teach only partial depravity? They may *say* that man is dead in sin, but they actually *believe* that there is a spark of goodness or a glimmer of divinity left in the soul. Beliefs of that kind devastate the Christian religion. If man is totally depraved, dead in sin, then he not only does not have any good remaining in him, but also cannot do anything to restore his soul.

Most evangelical preachers would probably affirm the doctrine of total depravity, but would not practice what they preach. Let me illustrate with the following conversation between a preacher and an unbeliever. The unbeliever said to the preacher, "I have asked Jesus to come into my life many times. Please pray that he will accept me." The preacher responded, "You do not have to wait for Christ to accept you. He is waiting for you to accept him. The decision is yours, not Christ's. He decided in favor of you when he died for you on the cross. Now you must decide for him. As soon as he sees that you believe in him and trust him, he will enter into your life." This example demonstrates how the denial of total depravity sets up the individual as sovereign in salvation. To deny total depravity is to affirm the autonomy of the human will. Ultimately, the denial of true doctrine and the affirmation of false doctrine destroy God's sovereignty. If God is not sovereign, then man assumes the place of deity. So what must the unconverted sinner do? What must the evangelist do? It is very simple. The unconverted sinner should "seek the Lord while He may be found." The sinner should hear the teaching and preaching of the gospel from the Bible. He should obey the law written on his heart. The evangelist must pray that God will change the person's heart, and then leave the rest of it to the Holy Spirit.

The challenge to Christians is to believe the doctrine of total depravity and have the same conviction that Professor

Sproul had when he lectured to his class. Is theological integrity important? Then believe, study, and teach the doctrine of total depravity, even when people say, "Surely God didn't mean it."

2

SOLA SCRIPTURA

KEITH A. MATHISON

One of the rallying cries of the sixteenth-century Reformation was the Latin slogan *sola Scriptura,* which means "by Scripture alone." This doctrine, the "formal principle" of the Reformation,[1] has been a great source of comfort and confidence for believers down through the centuries. Unfortunately, it has also been the source of some confusion. Among the ranks of professing evangelicals, the doctrine of *sola Scriptura* has been used as a justification for numerous schisms and every imaginable heresy. Taken out of its historical context and interpreted in accordance with modern philosophies and ideas, an appeal to *sola Scriptura* has often ceased to be an appeal to the ultimate authority of God's Word, and instead has become an appeal to the sovereign conscience of the individual reader of Scripture. What was once only a Roman Catholic caricature of the doctrine has all too often become the reality, and many have left the ranks of evangelical Christianity because they have mistakenly assumed that this indefensible distortion of the Reformation doctrine was the actual doctrine itself. In order to guard against such misunderstanding and better grasp the true nature of the doctrine of *sola Scriptura,* it is necessary to have a general understanding of the historical context within which the debate developed.[2]

HISTORICAL CONTEXT

The historical debate over the doctrine of *sola Scriptura* is often wrongly characterized in terms of a conflict between Scripture and tradition. It is actually a debate involving differing concepts of tradition. There have been, during the church's history, essentially four main views of tradition. The first view, which has been termed "Tradition I" by Heiko Oberman, is a "one-source" theory of revelation, which sees the content of Scripture and tradition as identical.[3] According to this understanding of Scripture and tradition, the apostolic doctrine, which had been orally preached for decades after the death of Christ, was eventually written down in the books of the New Testament. This New Testament Scripture, along with the Old Testament, is the sole source of inspired revelation, and it is to be interpreted by the Church within the context of the apostolic rule of faith. The second view, which has been termed "Tradition II," is a "two-source" theory of revelation. According to this idea, Scripture and tradition are two equally authoritative and supplementary sources of divine revelation. On this view, the content of Scripture and tradition are *not* identical. The third view, which may be termed "Tradition III," understands the real source of revelation to be the living magisterium (teaching office) of the church. A final view, which may be termed "Tradition 0" (or *solo Scriptura*), rejects any role for tradition in any sense and argues that every individual is able to interpret Scripture correctly for himself according to his own private judgment, apart from the church, the creeds, and any other human help. In order to understand the doctrine of *sola Scriptura,* we must understand where it fits in the context of the long-standing debate over the proper understanding of tradition.

Church historians agree on how the church of the first three centuries understood the source of authority.[4] The early Fathers generally understood tradition to be the body of doctrine that had been committed to the church by Jesus and his apostles, whether orally or in writing. The content of this body of doctrine was the same, regardless of the form in which it was communicated. For the first few decades of the church's existence, this apostolic doctrine was communicated orally. There was no written New Testament at this point in time. Soon, however, the apostles began to commit their doctrine to writing in the Gospels and Epistles of the New Testament.

The New Testament, then, was the inscripturation of the apostolic proclamation. It was the *same* apostolic proclamation that had previously been preached orally. Together with the Old Testament, it was the church's source of divine revelation, and it was the sole doctrinal authority. The early Christians also believed that this written Scripture was to be interpreted in and by the church within the context of the general rule of faith taught by the apostles. At this early point in history, however, there is no indication that the Fathers believed that they had recourse to any second source of revelation that contained things not found in the New Testament. In other words, in the first three centuries, the church taught the concept of tradition described above as Tradition I.

The first hints of a two-source concept of revelation (Tradition II) begin to be observed in the writings of certain fourth-century church fathers. Such a view is strongly suggested in the writings of John Chrysostom, for example, and is possibly suggested in the writings of Basil and Augustine. There is good evidence, however, that neither Basil nor Augustine actually intended to teach a two-source view. Unfortunately, however, the hints of such a concept in the writings of these influential theologians ensured it a place in the thinking of the later medieval church.[5]

The general consensus of the early church remained the consensus throughout most of the Middle Ages. In other words, although there were some adherents of an undeveloped form of Tradition II in the early medieval era, most Christian theologians continued to adhere to a form of Tradition I. Due to changing circumstances, however, we begin to see the development of a full-fledged two-source theory of revelation in the writings of the twelfth-century canon lawyers. One of the primary reasons for such a development was the gradual rejection of allegorical hermeneutical methods in favor of more historical and grammatical methods of biblical interpretation. Many medieval doctrines and practices that had been defended from Scripture on the basis of an allegorical method of interpretation were indefensible if Scripture was interpreted more literally. In order to defend the apostolicity of some of these doctrines and practices, a second source of apostolic revelation was posited. Appeal was then made to the writings of early Fathers such as Basil and Augustine to support this view.

This development toward a two-source theory of revelation reached its apex in the thought of the fourteenth-century theologian William of Ockham. He is arguably the first medieval theologian to delineate a fully developed two-source theory.[6] From the fourteenth century onward, we witness the parallel development of two concepts of tradition. Many continued to uphold the Tradition I concept, insisting that although the Scriptures must be interpreted in and by the church within the context of the rule of faith, those Scriptures are the sole source of authoritative revelation. Others just as forcefully maintained the existence of an authoritative extrascriptural source of revelation (Tradition II). It is within the context of this ongoing debate that the Protestant Reformation of the sixteenth century must be understood.

Men like Martin Luther and John Calvin did not create a new doctrine when they began to combat the tyranny and apostasy of the Roman Catholic Church with a call to the doctrine of *sola Scriptura*. The classical Reformers were, in fact, calling the church back to its earlier teaching, back to a one-source concept of revelation, back to Tradition I. They asserted that Scripture was the sole source of divine revelation, and they denied the existence of a supplementary source. They also asserted that Scripture was to be interpreted in and by the church, in accordance with the ancient rule of faith, as summarized in the Christian creed. For example, Martin Luther, in a letter on the doctrine of the real presence of Christ in the Eucharist, wrote the following:

This article moreover has been clearly believed and held from the beginning of the Christian Church to this hour—a testimony of the entire holy Christian Church, which, if we had nothing besides, should be sufficient for us. For it is dangerous and terrible to hear or believe anything against the united testimony, faith, and doctrine, of the entire holy Christian Church, as this hath been held now 1,500 years, from the beginning, unanimously in all the world. Whoso now doubted thereon, it is even the same as though he believed in no Christian Church, and he condemneth thus not only the entire holy Christian Church as a damnable heresy, but also Christ himself and all the apostles and prophets, who have established and powerfully attested this article, where we say, "I believe in a holy Christian Church"; Christ namely, Matthew 28:20: "Lo I am with you always, even to the end of the world"; and Paul, 1 Timothy 3:15: "The Church of God, which is the pillar and ground of the truth."[7]

Of course, this same Luther also said about Holy Scripture, "My conscience is captive to the Word of God." But Luther's words before the Diet of Worms should not be interpreted in isolation from the other things he said on the subject of authority. When all of his writings are considered, it becomes clear that he held to a form of Tradition I.

The debate between adherents of Tradition I and adherents of Tradition II had been ongoing since the twelfth century, and both positions had been held within the church, but the Reformation widened the gap between the two views. The classical Reformers, such as Martin Luther and John Calvin, called the church back to Tradition I, the position of the early church. In response, their Roman Catholic opponents became more adamant in the proclamation of Tradition II. Eventually the two concepts were no longer able to coexist within the same ecclesiastical communion. Also, at the same time that this debate was taking place, a more radical group of Reformers began to proclaim a new concept of tradition.

Unlike the classical Reformers, the radical Reformers took a wholly negative approach to tradition. As Alister McGrath explains, according to the radicals, "every individual had the unfettered right to interpret Scripture in whatever manner seemed right to him or her."[8] The radical Reformers believed that the classical Reformers had not gone far enough in their application of the principle of *sola Scriptura*. According to the radical Reformers, the classical Reformers were making a mistake by continuing to adhere to the creedal formulations of the ancient church. The view of the radical Reformers, which we have described above as Tradition 0, or *solo Scriptura,* places the private judgment of the individual above the corporate judgment of the church. According to adherents of Tradition 0, Scripture is not merely the sole inspired and infallible authority; it is the sole authority altogether. It is important to understand that two completely different views emerged from the Reformation, and that Tradition 0 was not the position held by such men as Martin Luther and John Calvin.

Within the Roman Catholic Church, the two-source view of revelation (Tradition II) was eventually made official church dogma at the Council of Trent. For the next three hundred years, it was the position taught by official representatives and teachers of the Roman Church. But during the last century and a half, a new view has begun to emerge within the Roman Church. Oberman explains the development:

> The two notions of living development and binding authority of the teaching office of the Church to which Cardinal Newman and systematic theologian Jos. Scheeben (d. 1888) contributed in the same century, together with the declaration of the dogmas (1854) of the immaculate con-

ception of the Virgin Mary, of (1870) the definition of papal infallibility and of (1950) the pronouncement of the bodily assumption of the immaculate Virgin, have led in our time to a reconsideration of the relation of the *Magisterium* as active tradition to the so-called sources of Revelation as the objective tradition. Notwithstanding appearances the debate on the relation of Scripture and extra-biblical tradition has lost some of its former urgency. A Tradition III concept is in the process of being developed by those who tend to find in the teaching office of the Church the one and only source for revelation. Scripture and tradition are then not much more than historical monuments of the past.[9]

In other words, Rome is gradually moving toward a one-source concept of revelation, but the one source of revelation is the Roman magisterium. In practice, what this means is that whatever Rome *now* teaches is, by definition, the tradition of the church. This is, of course, the logical implication of the doctrine of papal infallibility, but it is also a virtual declaration of autonomy that places all authority in the hands of the "magisterium of the moment."

Within the Protestant church, especially in the United States, the doctrine of *solo Scriptura* (Tradition 0) became the rallying cry for nineteenth-century sectarians and theological liberals.[10] The separatist Christian Movement of Alexander Campbell, for example, applied the democratic American philosophy to Christianity and argued for a "religion of, by, and for the people."[11] The Christian Movement called for the exaltation of the individual conscience over the collective conscience of the church. It also called for theological innovation and the rejection of traditional theology. It called for every person to read the Bible as if no one had ever seen its pages before and apart from the mediation of any clergy, creeds, or theology.[12]

Liberal Christians of the nineteenth century used the same understanding of Scripture to promote their own theological innovations.[13] The Universalist minister A. B. Grosh, for example, argued that the Bible "is our only acknowledged creed book." The liberal theologian Simeon Howard argued that men should "lay aside all attachment to human systems, all partiality to names, councils and churches, and honestly inquire, 'what saith the Scriptures.'" The Unitarian Noah Worchester argued that Christians would reject the doctrine of the Trinity if they would simply study the Scriptures apart from the creeds of the church. The liberal clergyman Charles Beecher denounced what he called "creed power" and called for "the Bible, the whole Bible, and nothing but the Bible." The conservative Reformed theologian Samuel Miller responded to this liberal phenomenon by pointing out "that the most zealous opposers [of creeds] have generally been latitudinarians and heretics."[14] He was right. The distortion of *sola Scriptura* that we have referred to as Tradition 0 was used during the nineteenth and early twentieth centuries to deny every fundamental doctrine of Christianity, including the Trinity, the deity of Christ, the inspiration of Scripture, the Resurrection, and the Atonement.[15]

Unfortunately, this same phenomenon continued unabated in the twentieth century. Within much of evangelicalism today, the classical Reformation doctrine of *sola Scriptura* has been essentially rejected in favor of the individualistic doctrine of *solo Scriptura*. Tradition 0 has largely supplanted Tradition I. Today, many professing evangelicals have taken up the mantle of the late nineteenth-century modernists and continue to use *solo Scriptura* to promote old and new heresies alike. No essential doctrine of Christianity has escaped revision and outright rejection at the hands of those who have rejected the hermeneutical boundaries of apostolic Christianity in favor of the self-exalting authority of their own individual minds.[16]

The doctrine of the apostolic church was the doctrine we have described as Tradition I. According to this doctrine, Scripture is the sole source of revelation. Because of its unique character as the inspired word of the living God, it is the sole infallible authority for doctrine and practice. Yet Scripture must be interpreted within the hermeneutical boundaries of the apostolic rule of faith, and it must be interpreted in and by the church. The late medieval church had largely abandoned this idea in favor of Tradition II, a two-source concept of revelation. The Reformers called the church to return to Tradition I, using the language of *sola Scriptura*. Today both the Roman Catholic Church and much of the Protestant church have rejected *sola Scriptura* in favor of doctrines that result in different kinds of autonomy. The Roman Catholic Church has adopted a doctrine that results in the autonomy of its teaching office, and much of the Protestant church has adopted a doctrine that results in the autonomy of the individual Christian. Both are serious aberrations. The only doctrine that places final authority where it actually exists—in God and his Word—is the doctrine of *sola Scriptura*.

SCRIPTURE IS THE SOLE SOURCE OF REVELATION

As we have already observed, the modern debate over the doctrine of *sola Scriptura* has too often been wrongly framed as Scripture versus tradition. However, the real question is not whether we will teach a concept of tradition; the real question concerns *which* concept of tradition we will teach. We have briefly examined the four main options that have been suggested in the history of the church. Only one of these options—Tradition I—can make a plausible claim to be the teaching of the apostolic church. This is the doctrine that was proclaimed by the classical Reformers in the face of Roman Catholic theological and practical abuses. Using the slogan *sola Scriptura,* they called upon the church to return to the teaching of the early church. They insisted that Scripture was the sole source of revelation, that it was the final authoritative norm for doctrine and practice, that it was to be interpreted in and by the church, and that it was to be interpreted within the context of the rule of faith. In order to understand fully the classical Reformation (and apostolic) doctrine of *sola Scriptura,* it is necessary that we examine each aspect of this doctrine.

PERFECTION

The perfection of Scripture is essentially its completeness as a source of revelation.[17] Because Scripture is the Word of God, conservatives on all sides of the debate grant that it is perfect in the sense of being inspired. Proponents of Tradition II would deny that Scripture is perfect in the sense of its being a complete and adequate source of revelation. Wayne Grudem provides a helpful definition of the perfection of Scripture in his *Systematic Theology.* The perfection of Scripture means that Scripture "contained all the words of God he intended his people to have at each stage of redemptive history, and that it now contains everything we need God to tell us for salvation, for trusting him perfectly, and for obeying him perfectly."[18]

The perfection of Scripture is taught in numerous places throughout Scripture itself. In Deuteronomy 29:29, for example, Moses says, "The secret things belong to the LORD our God, but the things that are revealed belong to us and to our children forever, that we may do all the words of this law." The clear implication of Moses' words is that all revelation that is necessary for the people to be obedient to the law of God at this point in history was revealed, not to a select few, but to all of the people. That which is secret belongs to God. That which is revealed is revealed to all. Jesus makes a similar point in the story of the rich man and Lazarus (Luke 16:19–31). After the two men die, the rich man is suffering in torment. He begs Abraham to allow Lazarus to go to his brothers with a special revelation warning them of the fate that will befall them unless they repent of their wicked ways. Abraham's words to the rich man are revealing: "They have Moses and the Prophets; let them hear them" (16:29). The point is that everything necessary for their salvation may be found in the extant Scriptures. No second source of revelation is necessary. The apostle Paul emphasizes the same doctrine when he tells Timothy that the Scriptures "are able to make you wise for salvation through faith in Christ Jesus" (2 Tim. 3:15). All the revelation that we need for salvation may be found in Scripture. It is a perfect and complete source of revelation for the Christian church.

SUFFICIENCY

Although the sufficiency of Scripture and the perfection of Scripture are virtually identical concepts, it is necessary to discuss the sufficiency of Scripture separately because it has become the focus of much of the debate. In some cases,

Protestant authors have virtually identified the doctrine of *sola Scriptura* with the doctrine of the sufficiency of Scripture.[19] However, there is more to *sola Scriptura* than the sufficiency of Scripture. If we reduce the doctrine of *sola Scriptura* to the doctrine of sufficiency, we seriously undermine the entire doctrine.

Evangelical adherents of Tradition 0 will deny that the classical Reformation doctrine of Tradition I is the doctrine of *sola Scriptura* because Tradition I insists that the church and the rule of faith are also necessary parts of the doctrine. However, an illustration of why this charge is false may prove helpful. Protestant evangelicals have often made it clear, when discussing the doctrine of *sola fide,* that justification is by faith alone, but not by a faith that is alone.[20] We are justified by faith alone, but a faith that does not produce spiritual fruit is a dead faith that cannot save. Similarly, our final authority is Scripture alone, but not a Scripture that is alone. Scripture is the only source of revelation. Scripture alone is inspired. Scripture alone is inherently infallible. Scripture alone is the supreme normative standard. But Scripture does not exist in a vacuum. It was given to the church within the context of the apostolic gospel. Scripture alone is the final authoritative standard, but it is a standard that must be interpreted and preached by the church. When Scripture is interpreted apart from that context, it ceases to function properly as the final authoritative standard. Scripture is certainly sufficient, but it is only sufficient for certain things. It cannot read itself. It cannot preach itself. It cannot interpret itself.[21] That is the duty and responsibility of the church. To insist on this is no more a denial of *sola Scriptura* than an insistence on living faith is a denial of *sola fide.*

SCRIPTURE IS THE FINAL AUTHORITATIVE NORM

A vital element of the Reformation doctrine of *sola Scriptura* is the assertion that Scripture alone is the final and authoritative norm for Christian faith and practice. The Reformation doctrine of *sola Scriptura* does not assert that Scripture is the only authority at all. That idea belongs to the concept of Tradition 0. There are other authorities that are subordinate to Scripture, but Scripture is the only inspired and inherently infallible authority, and therefore it is the only final and authoritative norm.

INSPIRATION

In order to demonstrate the normative authority of Scripture, it is necessary to begin with a discussion of Scripture's inspiration. In 2 Timothy 3:16, the apostle Paul writes, "All Scripture is breathed out by God and profitable for teaching, for reproof, for correction, and for training in righteousness." In many English translations, the Greek word translated "breathed out" (*theopneustos*) is translated "inspired." It literally means "God-breathed." The basic meaning of the doctrine of inspiration is that the words of Scripture are the very words of God. As Charles Hodge explains,

> On this subject the common doctrine of the church is, and ever has been, that inspiration was an influence of the Holy Spirit on the minds of certain select men, which rendered them the organs of God for the infallible communication of his mind and will. They were in such a sense the organs of God, that what they said God said.[22]

Inspiration was necessary in order to guard the revelation of God from the inherent propensity of fallen man to err. The prophets and apostles were not inherently infallible human beings (cf. Gal. 2:11–13). However, when God used them to communicate his revelation, they spoke "as they were carried along by the Holy Spirit" (2 Peter 1:21).

The most important point here is that the apostle Paul teaches that "all" Scripture is inspired or God-breathed. Every word of Scripture was given by the inspiration of God, so the whole of Scripture is the very word of the living God. Inspiration is a unique characteristic that belongs to Scripture alone. No other purported source of revelation can claim this attribute. The writings of the church fathers are not inspired. The creeds of the church are not inspired. Inspiration is not even claimed by Rome for the *ex cathedra* pronouncements of the pope. In other words, there is a distinction between that which is inspired (Scripture) and that which is not (everything else). The "God-breathed" nature of Scripture leads to another important point—the infallibility of Scripture.

INFALLIBILITY

Because Scripture alone is inspired, or God-breathed, it alone is inherently infallible. Infallibility is the inability to err. Infallibility entails inerrancy—the actual absence of error. Scripture alone can plausibly claim full and complete inspiration; therefore, Scripture alone can plausibly claim full and complete infallibility and inerrancy.

Both Roman Catholicism and Eastern Orthodoxy claim infallibility for the church, and Rome adds to this the claim of papal infallibility. However, neither communion claims full or complete infallibility for the church or the pope. Neither communion claims that a person can open any official church document or papal decree at random and be absolutely assured that he is reading an error-free statement. In fact, the Roman

45

doctrine of papal infallibility explicitly limits this infallibility to those decrees that meet certain strictly defined criteria. Thus, both the Roman church and the Orthodox church actually teach a version of limited infallibility. The problem with this concept, however, is that whether it is applied to the church or the pope, it is self-contradictory. Something is either infallible or it isn't. The presence of even one error rules out the possibility of infallibility. Limited or partial infallibility is simply fallibility.

Infallibility requires inerrancy—the absence of error—and so the presence of even one error negates any claim to infallibility. It is universally acknowledged that one may find numerous errors in the writings of the church and in the writings of the popes. It is therefore impossible to claim for either the church or the pope an inherent, unconditional infallibility. But neither Rome nor the Orthodox church claims an inherent, unconditional infallibility. The problem with this is that there is no other kind of infallibility. By definition, infallibility is absolute. Only an absolute authority can be infallible, and the only absolute authority is God himself. Since Scripture is the very word of this one absolute authority, it alone can claim inherent, unconditional infallibility. One may turn randomly to any part of Scripture and be assured that one is reading an error-free statement. The same cannot be said of any other writing on this earth.

AUTHORITY

Because Scripture is the God-breathed and therefore infallible word of the living God, it carries absolutely unique authority—the authority of God himself. Rome has claimed that Scripture derives its existence and therefore its authority from the church. Classical Protestantism, on the other hand, has argued that Scripture derives its existence and therefore its authority from divine inspiration. Rome has confused the recognition of authority with the actual conferral of authority, and in so doing it has failed to recognize that the *word* of God is authoritative by its very nature as the word *of God*.

God has within himself, by virtue of who he is, an absolutely unique and sovereign authority. No man or institution (including the church) can claim to have an authority equal to or greater than that of almighty God. Man is not God and does not have the authority of God. Because Scripture is inspired or God-breathed, it is the very word of the uniquely sovereign and authoritative God. It is God's revelation, his speech, his words, his voice. As the voice of almighty God, Scripture carries all of the authority of God himself. That being the case, it is impossible for any man or institution to claim to have an authority equal to or higher than Scripture. That would be equivalent to claiming an authority equal to or greater than that of God himself. No church explicitly claims to have such authority, yet some churches claim that the church has authority that is prior to and greater than that of Scripture. What these churches do not seem to understand is that a claim to greater authority than that of Scripture is a claim to greater authority than that of God. Such a claim is nothing short of blasphemy. If Scripture truly is the word of almighty God, then the issue of final authority is settled.

SUPREME NORMATIVITY

The unique, final, and infallible authority of Scripture necessarily means that it stands as the church's supreme norm and standard. This was one of the key elements of the early Protestant formulation of the doctrine of *sola Scriptura*. Scripture alone is the *norma absoluta*—the "absolute norm"—because

Scripture alone is God-breathed. Scripture's supreme norma-
tivity for the faith and practice of the church is nothing more
than the logical corollary of its inspiration, infallibility, and
unique authority. If Scripture is the inspired word of God
himself, if it is completely and unconditionally infallible, if it
carries the very authority of God himself by virtue of its being
his word, then it is self-evident that it is the church's supreme
norm and standard. Nothing else could be. No other proposed
norm or standard can claim the same attributes for itself. The
writings of the Fathers are not God-breathed. The creeds are
not God-breathed. The church does not speak with the inherent authority of God himself. Scripture is absolutely unique in
this respect, and it is for this reason that "Scripture alone"—
sola Scriptura—is the supreme norm and standard for the
church's faith and practice.

THE CHURCH

Another element of the doctrine of *sola Scriptura* (as opposed to *solo Scriptura*) is the idea that Scripture is to be interpreted in and by the church within the context of the rule of
faith. This is the fundamental difference between Tradition I
(the position of the early church and the classical Reformers)
and Tradition 0 (the position of the radical Reformers and
most modern evangelicals). The doctrine of *sola Scriptura* asserts that Scripture is truth (John 17:17), and that the church
is the pillar and ground of the truth (1 Tim. 3:15). There is,
therefore, a necessary relationship between the Spirit-inspired
Word of God and the Spirit-indwelt people of God.

To assert that Scripture is the only inspired and inherently
infallible authority, and that it is the final and supreme norm,

does not in any way rule out the necessity or reality of secondary authorities. The church is one such authority. The church was established by Jesus Christ (Matt. 16:18); the church is given the authority to teach and disciple the nations (Matt. 28:18–20); the church is the instrument through which God makes the truth of his word known (Eph. 3:10). It is only within the church that Scripture can be interpreted correctly. The church is the human agency with the authority and ability to speak. The Scripture contains the content of what she is to speak. The church is necessary because the Bible cannot preach itself, and without the Bible, the church has nothing to say.

The rightful authority of the church does not remove the right and responsibility of the individual Christian to read and study Scripture. It does, however, challenge the modern notion of individualism. While each individual may and must read and study Scripture in order that his conscience may be bound by the Word of God, ecclesiastical authority cannot rest in the judgment of each individual member of the church. The private judgment of individuals cannot replace the corporate judgment of the covenant community of God.

The corporate judgment of the covenant community of God normally operates through those who have been given gifts of teaching and leadership in the church (cf. Matt. 18:17; Acts 15:6–35; 1 Cor. 12:28; Eph. 4:11–13). These spiritual gifts, given to certain members of the church, carry with them a level of authority that is not shared by every member of the church (Heb. 13:17). While their authority is not infallible, it is certainly real. It is necessary to remember that there is a profound difference between the internal court of conscience and the external ecclesiastical court. The inward court of individual conscience cannot be bound by anything other than the

Word of God, but the church does have real binding authority in the external ecclesiastical court. This authority has been
given to the church in order that she may preserve the unity
of the faith and reject the errors of heretics.

THE RULE OF FAITH

The doctrinal authority that has been given to the church
is intimately connected to the creeds of the church and the
rule of faith. The rule of faith was a summary of apostolic
doctrine that was preserved by the church, taught to new cat-
echumens, and eventually inscripturated in complete form by
the apostles in the canonical books of the New Testament. Its
summary form was eventually expressed in writing in the
early creeds of the church. This rule of faith functioned as a
standard hermeneutical context for the church in the first
decades and centuries following the death of the apostles. The
church was able to recognize heretics because they did not interpret Scripture in the context of this rule of faith. In other
words, they did not interpret Scripture within the context of
the Christian faith.

The rule of faith is a necessary aspect of the doctrine of *sola
Scriptura* because the alternative is hermeneutical chaos. Any
person who has been a Christian for more than a few days is
aware that there are numerous competing interpretations of
Scripture. There are disagreements and debates on virtually
every major issue. How are these disputes to be resolved? If
we adopt the individualistic doctrine of Tradition 0, it is not
possible to settle any debate because the final authority is each
individual. Each individual decides for himself and by himself
which arguments are stronger. If the next person judges dif-

ferently, who determines which of them is correct? Within the context of Tradition 0, no one does. This is one of the main reasons why Tradition 0 has led to endless division within the church.

Without the church's rule of faith, there is no possible way even to begin resolving the multitude of doctrinal questions. The rule of faith that served as the hermeneutical context for the early church, when she was under attack from every direction, must regain its rightful place in our modern hermeneutical endeavors. Without it, the task of hermeneutics is nothing more than a futile exercise in relativism and subjectivism. The rule of faith, which is succinctly set forth in the Nicene Creed and Chalcedonian Definition, simply cannot be abandoned in the name of modern individualism. If these creeds have no authority, then there are no essential or fundamental doctrines of the Christian faith. The essential doctrines of the Christian faith would be determined by each individual on the basis of his own subjective opinion. In other words, the rejection of the subordinate authority of the creeds destroys the possibility of a coherent Christianity.

CONCLUSION

The doctrine of *sola Scriptura* has been under attack for centuries. Many Protestants are aware of the Roman Catholic Church's rejection of this doctrine. Most Protestants are unaware, however, that most evangelicals have also rejected the doctrine of *sola Scriptura* by completely altering its definition. Rome has rejected the doctrine of *sola Scriptura* in favor of either Tradition II or Tradition III, while many evangelicals have rejected *sola Scriptura* in favor of Tradition 0. Both perversions of the doctrine of *sola Scriptura* are dangerous because both usurp the final, sovereign authority that belongs to God himself. The doctrine of Rome places final authority in the mind of the church, and the doctrine of evangelicalism places final authority in the mind of each individual. Both are declarations of autonomy. Only the doctrine of *sola Scriptura* (Tradition I) places final authority where it actually belongs—with God and his word. It is this doctrine that must be reclaimed and proclaimed by the church if she is to preach the gospel of Christ to a dying world.

3

UNCONDITIONAL ELECTION

W. ROBERT GODFREY

Huckleberry Finn—no doubt expressing the sentiments of Mark Twain and many others—did not
like church or sermons. He complained to Tom
Sawyer about life in the home of the widow Douglas: "I got to
go to church and sweat and sweat—I hate them onery sermons. I can't ketch a fly in there, I can't chaw. I got to wear
shoes all Sunday." But for Huck some sermons were more
"onery" than others: "Two of the toughest hours I ever did
spend was listening to a Presbyterian minister drone on about
pre-fore-destination."

Today sermons on predestination are rare. While Calvinists still affirm the doctrine, they often seem hesitant to teach
it or preach it. They know that many people find it hard to
understand and hard to accept. This doctrine of unconditional

election, however, is not hard to accept because of its complexity or obscurity. It is hard to accept because it so fundamentally challenges human pride. Election forces us to acknowledge that the entire work of salvation is God's work and his alone. We as human beings can make no contribution of any kind. What do we have to offer to God? Luther answered that question best: "only our sins."

How, then, can we understand and teach the doctrine of election? We will find our answers in two places for the purposes of this essay. First, we will look at one of the great systematic theological answers to our question, as presented at the historic Synod of Dort. Second, we will look at the way in which the apostle Paul presented the doctrine in the first chapter of his letter to the Ephesians. We begin with the Synod of Dort because it sought to summarize all the teaching of Scripture in its doctrinal formulation. We conclude with Paul to see how much of that teaching on predestination can be found in just one key chapter of Holy Scripture.

THE SYNOD OF DORT

The Synod of Dort met in the Dutch city of Dordrecht from November 1618 to May 1619. It was an international gathering of representatives from Reformed churches in England, Scotland, Switzerland, and Germany, as well as the Netherlands. This synod convened to respond to the serious challenge posed by the followers of James Arminius to historic Reformed theology. Arminius (who died in 1610) and his disciples in the Dutch Reformed Church had raised serious questions about five teachings of Calvinism: unconditional election, limited atonement, total depravity, irresistible grace,

54

and the perseverance of the saints. The leading theologians of the Reformed world assembled at the synod to answer and refute Arminian theology. The decisions of the Synod of Dort are known as the Canons (or rules) of Dort.

The first chapter of the Canons of Dort—usually called the First Head of Doctrine—deals with unconditional election. The authors of the Canons decided that they wanted to write their chapters and subordinate articles in language intended not just for theologians, but for the church as a whole. They desired to show that Reformed teaching was both clear and profitable for the life of the church. Each article of the First Head of Doctrine is written simply and pastorally. (Sometimes modern readers miss that character of the articles because the sentences are long. But the reader who looks at each section of each sentence will see that the meaning is clear.)

The authors of the Canons also wanted to refute the Arminian claim that the Reformed position was sectarian. They accomplished that refutation in each of the Heads of Doctrine by beginning with a Christian doctrine that was catholic and noncontroversial. They started with a doctrinal statement that Lutherans and Roman Catholics would accept as readily as the Reformed did. They then proceeded to show how the Reformed view flowed naturally and biblically from that catholic beginning. The articles in the First Head of Doctrine not only provide us with a fine statement of the doctrine, but also show us an effective way of teaching it.

Where to begin in teaching the doctrine of predestination is an important question. Some great theologians have begun with the mind of God in eternity. Such a choice is certainly legitimate, but it may seem remote and abstract to many Christians. The Canons begin with the all-too-familiar human problem of sin and alienation from God.

Article 1: As all men have sinned in Adam, lie under the curse, and are deserving of eternal death, God would have done no injustice by leaving them all to perish and delivering them over to condemnation on account of sin, according to the words of the apostle: "That every mouth may be stopped, and all the world may be brought under the judgment of God" (Rom. 3:19). And: "For all have sinned, and fall short of the glory of God" (Rom. 3:23). And: "For the wages of sin is death" (Rom. 6:23).

This first article makes clear that all men are sinners and that sin deserves everlasting punishment. In light of the original human rebellion against him, God was not obligated to save anyone. If he had sent every human being to hell, he would have acted justly. Sinners in themselves have no right to, or claim on, the mercy of God. This point is critical for answering the charge that election is unfair. If God had left all men in sin, he would not have been unfair.

Article 2: But in this the love of God was manifested, that He "sent his only begotten Son into the world, that whosoever believeth in him should not perish, but have eternal life" (I John 4:9; John 3:16).

The second article gives a brief summary of the gospel. God did not leave all humans in the misery and hopelessness of their fallen state. In his great love, God sent his own Son into the world to save sinners. This article does not specify the work of Jesus—a life of perfect obedience and a death as the sacrificial substitute for sinners—but shows that salvation is only in him. Sinners must look away from themselves and trust him. Those who trust the Son will have eternal life.

This article is also foundational to any correct understanding of election. One of the tragic caricatures of the doctrine is the idea that many people want to be saved, but can't be saved, because they are not elect. Article 2 makes crystal clear the Reformed teaching that everyone who truly believes in Jesus will be saved.

> **Article 3:** And that men may be brought to believe, God mercifully sends the messengers of these most joyful tidings to whom He will and at what time He pleases; by whose ministry men are called to repentance and faith in Christ crucified. "How then shall they call on him in whom they have not believed? And how shall they believe in him whom they have not heard? And how shall they hear without a preacher? And how shall they preach except they be sent?" (Rom. 10:14, 15).

Article 3 shows that the mercy of God is found not only in his sending his Son to save sinners, but also in his provision of preachers to take the message of salvation throughout the world. Here is another anticipation of objections that are often brought against predestination. Some ask: If God has determined all things from eternity, and if God works all things according to his will, why should Christians seek to make Christ known? The answer is that God uses means to accomplish his will. He uses those who speak the message of his Son. We must be active in making Christ known because that is the way in which God has chosen to work.

> **Article 4:** The wrath of God abides upon those who believe not this gospel. But such as receive it and embrace Jesus the Savior by a true and living faith are by Him delivered from

the wrath of God and from destruction, and have the gift of eternal life conferred upon them.

The fourth article makes clear that those who reject the gospel remain in the lost and hopeless condition that already characterizes their lives. Rejecting the gospel is a grievous sin, but it is one of many sins that alienate unbelievers from God. By contrast, those who believe the gospel receive its rich benefits. They are delivered from the wrath of God both in the present and for the future. In Christ, the blessing of eternal life is conferred upon them.

Article 5: The cause or guilt of this unbelief as well as of all other sins is no wise in God, but in man himself; whereas faith in Jesus Christ and salvation through Him is the free gift of God, as it is written: "By grace have ye been saved through faith; and that not of yourselves, it is the gift of God" (Eph. 2:8). Likewise: "To you it hath been granted in the behalf of Christ, not only to believe on him," etc. (Phil. 1:29).

As there are two kinds of people, unbelievers and believers, so there are two causes for their two conditions. Article 5 states that the cause of unbelief is in man, not in God. God does not give the gift of unbelief to sinners. Rather, sinners exercise their rebellious wills to resist God and reject his Son. By contrast, God does give the gift of faith. Since all sinners in themselves resist God, he must overcome that resistance and effectively give the gift of faith in his Son. Unbelievers have only themselves to blame for their unbelief. Believers have only God to thank for the wonderful gift of faith.

These first five articles present the common teaching of evangelical Protestants and at least most Roman Catholics.

They are intended to show the catholic character of Reformed Christianity and to refute common accusations thrown at the Reformed. They also set the stage for the inevitable question: Why do some receive the gift of faith and others not? Ultimately, only one of two answers is possible to that question. Some receive the gift of faith either because of something in themselves—some greater wisdom or goodness, some greater exercise of the will, some decision not to resist grace—or because of something in God.

> **Article 6:** That some receive the gift of faith from God, and others do not receive it, proceeds from God's eternal decree. "For known unto God are all his works from the beginning of the world" (Acts 15:18, A.V.). "Who worketh all things after the counsel of his will" (Eph. 1:11). According to which decree He graciously softens the hearts of the elect, however obstinate, and inclines them to believe; while He leaves the non-elect in His just judgment to their own wickedness and obduracy. And here is especially displayed the profound, the merciful, and at the same time the righteous discrimination between men equally involved in ruin; or that decree of election and reprobation, revealed in the Word of God, which, though men of perverse, impure, and unstable minds wrest it to their own destruction, yet to holy and pious souls affords unspeakable consolation.

Article 6 makes clear the Reformed teaching that some receive the gift of faith because of something in God. He has decided or decreed in eternity to give the gift to some and not to others. To give that gift, he must work effectively in the hearts of the elect, so that they will believe. God externally sends his Son to die for sinners and sends his preachers to make the

Son's salvation known. God also internally sends his Spirit to soften hearts and irresistibly move wills, so that his chosen ones will believe.

This article reminds us that predestination shows us the very character of God. In his leaving some sinners in their sin, he shows his righteousness and justice. In his giving the gift of faith to some sinners, he shows his love and mercy. To unbelievers, this doctrine is offensive and terrible. But to believers it provides unspeakable consolation.

In later articles of the Canons, the theme of the consolation of election is developed. We will look more at that theme later. But here we should briefly point out the nature of that consolation. Election assures believers that their salvation did not originate with them and does not finally depend on them. God planned their salvation in eternity and sent his Son to die for them. God sent preachers to them and placed his Spirit within them to give them the gift of faith. And he who began a good work in them will bring it to completion in the Day of our Lord Jesus Christ. Here is real comfort: God saves us from beginning to end. No one—not even I—can finally pluck me from the Savior's hand, if I belong to him.

> **Article 7:** Election is the unchangeable purpose of God, whereby, before the foundation of the world, He has out of mere grace, according to the sovereign good pleasure of His own will, chosen from the whole human race, which had fallen through their own fault from their primitive state of rectitude into sin and destruction, a certain number of persons to redemption in Christ, whom He from eternity appointed the Mediator and Head of the elect and the foundation of salvation. This elect number, though by nature neither better nor more deserving than others, but

with them involved in one common misery, God has decreed to give to Christ to be saved by Him, and effectually to call and draw them to His communion by His Word and Spirit; to bestow upon them true faith, justification, and sanctification; and having powerfully preserved them in the fellowship of His Son, finally to glorify them for the demonstration of His mercy, and for the praise of the riches of His glorious grace; as it is written: "Even as he chose us in him before the foundation of the world, that we should be holy and without blemish before him in love: having foreordained us unto adoption as sons through Jesus Christ unto himself, according to the good pleasure of his will, to the praise of the glory of his grace, which he freely bestowed on us in the Beloved" (Eph. 1:4, 5, 6). And elsewhere: "Whom he foreordained, them he also called: and whom he called, them he also justified: and whom he justified, them he also glorified" (Rom. 8:30).

This long seventh article is a summary statement, pulling together various elements of the doctrine, most of which are found elsewhere in the Canons. In each Head of Doctrine, one article is a complete statement of the doctrine, and that is what we find here in this article. Notice several key points. First, election is the unchangeable purpose of God. He will not change and cannot be frustrated. Election is a great certainty to the believer. Second, the only motive for God's choice is his good pleasure. God is not arbitrary in his choice, but he does please himself. His electing purpose asks us to trust him in who he is as well as in what he does. Third, God chooses specific individuals for life. He does not just choose certain categories of people or certain conditions for people to meet. He chooses individuals because individuals need salvation and without his saving work could never enter categories or meet conditions for salvation. Fourth, the individuals chosen for life cannot in any way boast about their election. They are not superior or more deserving than others. Rather, the truth of election should make the elect the humblest of people, overcome with the wonder of God's free favor shown to them. Fifth, this article reminds us that God does not just begin the process of salvation, but provides every element that we need for eternal life. From beginning to end, salvation is of the Lord.

Articles 8–18 of the First Head of Doctrine develop specific aspects of the doctrine of election. We do not need to look at each article here. But two further articles will help us grasp the doctrine of election more fully and usefully. One such article deals with assurance of election.

> **Article 12:** The elect in due time, though in various degrees and in different measures, attain the assurance of this their eternal and unchangeable election, not by inquisitively prying into the secret and deep things of God, but by observing in themselves with a spiritual joy and holy pleasure the infallible fruits of election pointed out in the Word of God— such as, a true faith in Christ, filial fear, a godly sorrow for sin, a hungering and thirsting after righteousness, etc.

The subject of assurance is itself a major doctrine with many aspects. Among Reformed theologians, some distinction has been drawn between different kinds of assurance: assurance of faith or salvation, assurance of election, and assurance of perseverance. Article 12 focuses particularly on assurance of election, noting that not all believers at all times equally experience a confident assurance that they are elect.

Such assurance is the proper blessing of believers, but may develop slowly.

Article 12 offers several pieces of practical advice on how to cultivate assurance of election. First, believers are not to try to know the mind of God directly. We have no access to the decree of God in itself. An attempt to know God apart from his revelation would be disastrous. Second, believers are to look to the Scriptures for assurance. The Bible tells us of the mercy of God in Jesus Christ and calls us to faith and repentance. Third, the Bible tells us what fruit of God's electing grace we can expect to see in ourselves. The fruit of grace is not mysterious or difficult to observe. This fruit is the basic character of the Christian life: true faith, awe of our heavenly Father, grief for sin, and a desire to be more holy. In other words, the evidence for being a Christian is the evidence for being elect, since only the elect are Christians.

The most difficult part of the doctrine of predestination for most people is the idea that some sinners are passed over in God's electing plan and left in their sins. This part of the doctrine is often called reprobation. Article 15 clearly states this aspect of predestination.

> **Article 15:** What peculiarly tends to illustrate and recommend to us the eternal and unmerited grace of election is the express testimony of sacred Scripture that not all, but some only, are elected, while others are passed by in the eternal decree; whom God, out of His sovereign, most just, irreprehensible, and unchangeable good pleasure, has decreed to leave in the common misery into which they have willfully plunged themselves, and not to bestow upon them saving faith and the grace of conversion; but, permitting them in His just judgment to follow their own ways, at last,

for the declaration of His justice, to condemn and punish them forever, not only on account of their unbelief, but also for all their other sins. And this is the decree of reprobation, which by no means makes God the Author of sin (the very thought of which is blasphemy), but declares Him to be an awful, irreprehensible, and righteous Judge and Avenger thereof.

This article shows the two elements of the doctrine of reprobation. The first is the passing over of some. Simply according to his good pleasure, God passes over some sinners, leaving them in their sin. They are responsible for their rebellion and sin, and God leaves them in their lost state. The second element is their condemnation and punishment. Those passed over are judged and punished for all their sins. They are not condemned because they have been passed over, but because they are sinners.

Reprobation illumines election by showing that the electing decree of God is purely his sovereign good pleasure. God is free to choose some and to pass over others without the slightest injustice to any sinner. His choosing for life shows his love and mercy; his leaving in sin shows his justice and righteousness. Reprobation, as passing over and as condemnation, reminds us that we live in a moral universe where there is a final Judge who will destroy sin and uphold righteousness. In a world of profound moral uncertainty, this message is vital. God is in no sense the author of sin, but is the Savior from sin and the Judge of sin.

Many have asked if this doctrine of reprobation is actually taught in the Bible, or whether it is the result of some kind of Reformed logic. If we look in the Bible, we find it there in several places. Jesus taught that Judas Iscariot was reprobate

(John 6:70–71; 13:18–19; 17:12). Peter taught the doctrine of reprobation (1 Peter 2:8), as did Jude (Jude 4). The fullest presentation of the teaching is in Romans 9.

In Romans 9, Paul faces a very difficult question: Can Christians really rely on the wonderful promises that they find in Romans 8, since those same promises seem to have failed for Israel? Paul is clear: "It is not as though the word of God had failed" for Israel (Rom. 9:6a). Paul shows that God's word has not failed, because all those who truly belong to Israel will be saved. The key point is that "not all who are descended from Israel belong to Israel" (9:6b). Paul teaches that within the nation of Israel, there are children of flesh and children of promise (9:8). Not all of the nation, therefore, are children of God. Physical descent is not enough. One must be a child of promise.

Paul then proves God's electing and reprobating purpose by giving several examples. First, in verses 7–9, he mentions the distinction between two individuals, Isaac and Ishmael—the one a child of promise, the other a child of the flesh. Then Paul refers to the case of Jacob and Esau (vv. 10–13). Paul makes his point strongly here. Jacob and Esau are twins, the sons of the same mother and father. Yet Jacob was a child of promise, and Esau was a child of the flesh. The discrimination between these two was a matter of election. It occurred before they were born, before they had done anything good or bad (v. 11). In reference to these two unborn persons, both equally corrupted in Adam's sin, but not yet differentiated by any personal sin, Paul cites Malachi: "Jacob I loved, but Esau I hated" (v. 13). Jacob is elect, and Esau is reprobate.

Some have tried to evade the clear teaching of the apostle at this point by claiming that Malachi 1:2–3 is talking about nations, not individuals. It is true that the primary focus of

Malachi is on the nations of Israel and Edom, but these nations reflect the character of their individual progenitors. Further, Paul in Romans 9 is clearly speaking of the individuals Jacob and Esau. He refers to them as the unborn children of Isaac and Rebecca. His whole point is about individuals, not nations.

After showing how God's election proves that the promise made to Israel has not failed, Paul goes on to face this question: Is election unjust (v. 14)? Paul's answer is that God is absolutely just when he discriminates between sinners, showing mercy to one and hardening another (v. 18). He gives the example of Moses and Pharaoh (vv. 15–17). Moses and Pharaoh, in themselves, were both sinners far from God. Was Moses chosen because he was better than Pharaoh? No. Only God's eternal, discriminating purpose can explain why sinful Moses received mercy and Pharaoh was hardened in his sin. Moses is elect, and Pharaoh is reprobate.

Paul has every opportunity to correct any misunderstanding about his teaching on election and reprobation when he entertains the question: "Why does he still find fault? For who can resist his will?" (v. 19). Does Paul answer by saying that God only reprobates those who resist his grace? No. He clearly asserts God's sovereign discrimination in election and reprobation: "Has the potter no right over the clay, to make out of the same lump one vessel for beauty and another for menial use?" (v. 21).

Romans 9 shows not only the clear biblical foundation for the doctrine of reprobation, but also its spiritual uses for the Christian. If we think about unbelievers in Israel or the betrayal of Judas, we may well ask, "Will I also betray my Lord and become an unbeliever? If a disciple like Judas can fall, may I not also fall?" Reprobation reminds us that those who reject Christ do not do so by their free will or sovereign decision. They do so according to God's eternal plan. They never had true faith. Their fall cannot discourage us because he who began a good work in us will bring it to completion.

The Canons of Dort not only teach us the Reformed doctrine of unconditional election, but also give us a helpful model for how to help others to understand the doctrine. They not only present the various elements of the doctrine, but also relate predestination to other elements of Christian truth. Most helpfully, they show us the usefulness of the doctrine to glorify God and to assure us of the certainty of our salvation.

EPHESIANS 1

Paul's approach to the doctrine of election in Ephesians 1 is quite different from that found in the Canons of Dort. The difference is not in the content of the doctrine, but in the way in which it is discussed. The authors of the Canons were intensely aware of the controversy that surrounded the doctrine and therefore presented it very carefully. Paul seems unaware of any controversy about the doctrine and uses it boldly and unself-consciously.

Paul begins his letter to the Ephesians with many familiar themes. He identifies himself as an apostle, speaks words of blessing for the saints of God, and praises God for his grace and goodness in Christ. He also writes about predestination. For Paul in Ephesians 1, election is not an incidental theme, but a central and unifying one. Like Romans 8, Ephesians 1 provides us with a golden chain of blessings from the Lord in which predestination is a crucial link.

In the few verses of Ephesians 1:1–6, Paul not only teaches us something of the content of the doctrine of election, but also teaches us how to speak about election. He speaks so naturally, so easily, so confidently about election that he challenges our tendency to be hesitant and fearful about speaking of it. He does not analyze every aspect of election in these verses. But he does show us something of what to speak, when to speak, and why to speak of predestination.

WHAT TO SPEAK

Paul begins his letter by celebrating God's action in choosing "us"—his own people—for salvation. Paul writes that God blesses his saints with every spiritual blessing (v. 3), that he chose us to be holy (v. 4), and that he predestined us to be adopted as his children (v. 5). Here Paul makes clear that God is the one, the only one, who chooses his people for salvation in Christ.

On what basis does this choosing take place? Does God choose us for salvation on the basis of something in us or only on the basis of his own will? Paul's answer is clear throughout these verses. First, he says that God chose us "before the foundation of the world" (v. 4). Since he chose us before we ever existed, that certainly implies that the reason for choosing us is in God and not in us. Second, Paul says that we were chosen in Jesus Christ (v. 5), in the one whom God loves (v. 6). In ourselves and on our own, God does not love us. He loves us only in Christ, the one who deserves his love. So we are chosen not for who we are, but for who Christ is. Third, Paul says that we are chosen in accordance with God's pleasure and will (v. 5). Paul uses the same word for "will" here that he used in verse 1 to describe himself as an apostle by the will of God. Paul, then, as Calvin said, is a mirror of election for us. As

Paul was chosen sovereignly to be an apostle, so we are chosen sovereignly for salvation. Paul was not chosen because of his superior goodness, for he was the chief of sinners. He was chosen only because of the merciful pleasure of God. Finally, Paul says that we are chosen freely (v. 6). God is free in election. He is not moved or compelled by anything external to himself. He simply chooses freely in accordance with his good pleasure.

God is utterly sovereign in election. His will, not ours, is determinative of salvation. Paul says nothing here about human free will as a factor in election or salvation. In fact, nowhere in the Bible is the phrase "free will" to be found. The idea of free will is never mentioned in connection with the salvation of sinners. God is always at the center of biblical discussions of election and salvation. Paul here and the Bible everywhere call us to be radically God-centered in our thinking. The doctrine of election is crucial to keep us theocentric.

WHEN TO SPEAK

When is it appropriate to speak of election? Even among those who believe in election, some seem to think that we should speak of predestination seldom, if ever. They treat election as our guilty secret—the less said the better. Others believe that we should talk about election, but only with mature Christians. Election, they say, is a doctrine that should be introduced only to those already well grounded in the faith.

Both of these approaches to election assume that election is a problem. But what kind of problem is election? Some say that it is a problem because it is mysterious and difficult. In some ways it may be, but so is the doctrine of the Trinity. Yet no true Christian would suggest that we should not teach all Christians about the Trinity.

Others say that election is a problem because it is controversial and unpopular. But so is the doctrine of hell. Yet Christians have rightly felt a responsibility to make clear the reality of final judgment and the horrors of everlasting punishment.

Still others say that election is a problem because it can so easily be misrepresented. Yet that is true of nearly every Christian doctrine. The biblical doctrine of justification, for example, has often been misrepresented as leading to an indifference to the pursuit of holiness. Yet we continue to believe that we must teach that we are justified by grace alone through faith alone.

Some have claimed to believe in election, while actually twisting it into a kind of fatalism and an excuse for being unconcerned with evangelism. One such group, known as the Hard Shell Baptists, even wrote hymns misusing the doctrine of election. One such hymn is purported to proclaim:

> We are the Lord's elected few;
> let all the rest be damned.
> There's room enough in Hell for you.
> We don't want Heaven crammed.

Such arrogant indifference to the lost is completely foreign to the genuine character of election.

A final reason why some see election as a problem—perhaps the most important reason—is that election strikes many as being unfair. Yet ordinary human standards of fairness conflict with several elements of Christian revelation. The doctrines of original sin and total depravity strike many as unfair, but are clearly taught in Scripture and are essential to the structure of Christian theology. The doctrine of the imputation of Christ's righteousness to sinners is not "fair" by most human standards. How can one person die to pay for the sins of another? But this doctrine is at the very heart of the gospel. Election may not always seem fair, but it is foundational to God's mercy to sinners.

The effect of not talking about election in the contemporary church has been disastrous. Today religion has often become more man-centered than medieval Christianity before the Reformation. At least in the Middle Ages the stress on human ability was focused on overcoming sin and meriting eternal life. Today, in too many churches, the focus is on using one's human potential to gain health, wealth, and happiness.

When we compare our relative silence about election with the Bible, we find that the Bible speaks frequently and frankly about it, just as we have seen in Ephesians 1. If we want to be biblical, we too must talk about it. And we must talk about it, as Paul did, with the biblical confidence that election is a solution, not a problem. Election is the solution because it glorifies God at every point in salvation and draws us away from ourselves to God.

We must, of course, speak about election in a clear, sensitive, and careful manner. As Calvin said in a sermon on this passage, "We know that our wisdom ought always to begin with humility."[1] But our humility should not lead us to silence, but rather to imitate Paul in his joyous expression of God's electing love.

WHY TO SPEAK

Paul speaks of election in Ephesians 1 because it glorifies God (v. 6). Election glorifies God because it shows that the work of salvation at every point is God's work. He originates the plan of salvation for each one of the elect in eternity. He sends his Son to die for those elect ones. He draws elect sinners by his irresistible Spirit to faith in his Son.

The glory of God's saving work leads us to praise him. Our minds in the first place should not focus on our needs or on our strengths, but should break into thanksgiving to God for all he has done. As Paul begins his letter to the Ephesians with a long prayer of praise, so praise and adoration should be a more prominent feature of our lives. As Calvin so powerfully put it in his sermon, "All who would do away with God's predestination or are loth to hear it spoken of, thereby show themselves to be mortal enemies of God's praise."[2]

We should also speak of election because it is a constituent part of our assurance of salvation. Election reminds us that any grace that is present in us comes from God, and that he will complete in us the work that he has begun. If we are in Christ, it is because we are elect. We know that we are elect and are strengthened in faith by contemplating Jesus. Again, as Calvin said, "Jesus Christ is the mirror in which God beholds us when he wishes to find us acceptable to himself. Likewise, on our side, he is the mirror on which we must cast our eyes and look, when we desire to come to the knowledge of our election."[3] When we look to Christ in faith, we see God's love and mercy and know that we are elect.

Reformed believers today are tempted to see the doctrine of election as a peculiar, "onery," and perhaps sectarian notion. We must remember that great theologians from Augustine to Thomas Aquinas to Martin Luther believed in predestination. All the great Reformed theologians have taught this doctrine clearly and summarized it in our great confessional documents, such as the Westminster Confession and the Canons of Dort. They knew and we must know that election is a glorious truth of God's Word with great practical importance for the life of the individual Christian and of the church. Let us continue to be biblical and speak freely of God's electing work.

4

SOLA FIDE

SINCLAIR B. FERGUSON

Justification by grace alone (*sola gratia*) through faith alone (*sola fide*) has stood at the center of evangelical theology ever since Martin Luther's famous insistence that the church stands or falls with this doctrine. While his younger contemporary, John Calvin, employed the concept of faith-union with Christ as the more all-embracing concept, he too could write of justification:

> This is the main hinge on which religion turns, so that we devote the greater attention and care to it. For unless you first of all grasp what your relationship to God is, and the nature of his judgment concerning you, you have neither a foundation on which to establish your salvation, nor one on which to build piety toward God.[1]

Thus, Reformed theology has echoed Luther's judgment that justification is ours *sola fide*. Indeed, defending Luther's emphasis on the *sola,* Calvin wrote with vigor against Rome, "Not only by a false but by an obviously ridiculous shift they insist upon excluding this adjective [i.e., *alone*]."[2]

But what does it mean that we are justified by faith alone? To unpack this, we need to reflect on both the nature of justification and the character of faith.

JUSTIFICATION

The Westminster divines declared that justification is "an act of God's free grace, wherein he pardoneth all our sins, and accepteth us as righteous in his sight, only for the righteousness of Christ imputed to us, and received by faith alone."[3]

Spelling this out more fully, justification involves both a negative aspect (pardon of sins) and a positive aspect (being counted righteous by God). This righteous standing is, according to the New Testament, eschatological (i.e., it is the judgment of the Last Day brought forward into the present) and final (i.e., it will never be reversed). It becomes ours through Jesus Christ, whom God has made our sin, and in whom we become the righteousness of God (1 Cor. 1:30; 2 Cor. 5:21). His righteousness is imputed, or counted, to us; in his righteousness we are righteous before God. We are thus "justified by his [God's] grace as a gift, through the redemption that is in Christ Jesus whom God put forward as a propitiation by his blood to be received by faith . . . so that he might be just and the justifier of him who has faith in Jesus" (Rom. 3:24–26 ESV).

How does this take place? Paul explains that Jesus Christ rose again for our justification (Rom. 4:25). The resurrection vindicates or justifies Jesus Christ as one counted righteous by God. In Paul's later statement, that Christ "was manifested in the flesh, vindicated [justified] by the Spirit, seen by angels, proclaimed among the nations, believed on in the world, taken up in glory" (1 Tim. 3:16 ESV), the Resurrection is similarly viewed as a vindication or justification by the Spirit. As the Last Adam, the Second Man, he was made sin for us, bore our guilt, sustained our punishment, and exhausted sin's power. He died to sin once for all and now is freed or justified from it (Rom. 6:10; cf. 6:7). In the Resurrection, God indicated that he counted Jesus righteous—how could he righteously do anything else?—since his Son was indeed righteous!

The implication of this for those who are "in Christ" is as startling as it is obvious: united to Christ as our substitute-representative, we share in his justification. We too are justified, counted as righteous before God. Indeed, to put it boldly, *we are as righteous before God as Jesus Christ himself is*—because it is in him, and with his righteousness, that we are righteous. Our righteousness *is* his righteousness; his righteousness *is* our righteousness!

To appreciate the significance of this we must explore the idea of justification a little more fully.

BIBLICAL BACKGROUND

In the Old Testament, central to the idea of righteousness (*tsedaqah*) is its covenant orientation. God's righteousness is his complete consistency with himself in the glory of his perfect being, and is expressed in the consistency between all his acts and the covenant declarations in which he has described and pledged himself to his people. Righteousness is his absolute integrity to his own character and to the covenant in which he expresses it. This covenant context explains why his righteousness can be expressed in either condemnation or salvation.[4]

Against this background, the righteous person is one who is rightly related to God through his covenant—a covenant that implies judgment on the unfaithful, but gracious and merciful provisions for sinners who trust in God's promises. Since all are sinners (Rom. 3:20ff.), the righteous man is not someone who is morally impeccable, but someone who, through these covenant provisions, has a right standing, status, and relationship with God. This explains Luther's vivid notion that the Christian is *simul justus et peccator* (righteous and yet at the same time a sinner).

Elijah is an obvious Old Testament illustration. His fervent prayers were effectual because he was a righteous man (James 5:16–17). Elijah was by no means sinless, but his relationship with God was grounded in the provisions of covenant grace and came to expression in his trust in God's covenant word and his obedience to his covenant commands. His praying was an expression of his faithfulness to the covenant promises and trust that God would bring to pass his covenant threats.[5]

The same was true of Abraham, who was accounted righteous by faith (Gen. 15:6; James 2:23). But James can also speak of the fulfillment of that "justification" in the way that Abraham was *"considered righteous* [justified] for what he did when he offered his son Isaac on the altar"* (James 2:21). In that act of obedience, Abraham acted in a righteous way, that is, in a manner consistent with absolute trust in the covenant God and his promise (cf. Rom. 4:20–24). James's point is not that Abraham's justification was rooted in his obedience, but that the obedient act of a justified man is in fact righteous (covenantally consistent), and thus that Abraham was appropriately "considered righteous" in doing it.

Therefore, when the Bible speaks about "justifying," it is not the creating of sinlessness that is in view, but rather the recognizing of a right relationship in the context of the covenant. To legitimate that right relationship *with sinners,* a covering over of sin by substitutionary sacrifice was essential (cf. Rom. 3:25). By means of the sacrifice of an impeccable animal in the Mosaic economy, God pointed his covenant people forward to the reality of an impeccable incarnate sacrifice as alone adequate to bear the weight of the exchange (Heb. 9:6–14; 10:1ff.).

Justification (considering or counting righteous), then, belongs to the world of relationship to God's norm, expressed in his own character-revealing covenantal demands. This sense is most frequently illustrated in biblical usage in the context of legal relationships. Three examples will suffice to make the point:

1. The Old Testament verb *tsadaq,* used in the causative (Hiphil: *hitsdiq*), means "to justify," being the antithesis of "to condemn": "When men have a dispute, they are to take it to court and the judges will decide the case, acquitting [justifying] the innocent and condemning the guilty" (Deut. 25:1). Here, clearly, only a declarative, constitutive sense of the verb is appropriate. To condemn is not to create a subjective moral condition of sin, but to constitute a relationship of guilt with respect to the norm (the law). This in turn leads to condemnation.

Similarly, Proverbs 17:15 speaks of God's hatred of justifying the guilty and condemning the innocent. If justification meant moral transformation, then Proverbs should commend, rather than condemn, such activity! To justify someone is, therefore, to constitute a person in a right relationship with respect to the norm (here, the law).

77

2. *Justify* carries a declarative sense in Job 32:2: "Elihu . . . became very angry with Job for justifying himself rather than God." The only possible sense in which God could be envisaged as being justified by Job is in a declarative sense. God is righteous, and he ought to be declared to be righteous. Similarly, when the tax collectors "justify" God, that justification is declarative (Luke 7:29; similarly Ps. 51:4, cited in Rom. 3:4).

3. Scripture uses the language of justification in connection with Christ's resurrection (cf. 1 Tim. 3:16, discussed above). There was, of course, a transformation involved in Jesus' resurrection, but it was not ethical in character. Rather, the physical transformation was itself the divine indication that Christ was declared, counted, or recognized to be righteous by God.

The connection between Christ's justification and ours underlines the significance of this statement. If Christ's justification in the Resurrection is the basis for our justification in union with him, then our justification will share the same declarative quality as his.

In passing, it is worth noting here—as Calvin saw so clearly[6]—that the role of union with Christ in our salvation safeguards the Reformation doctrine of justification from the twofold Roman Catholic criticism that the evangelical view of justification is a legal fiction and that it inevitably leads to moral indifference. In fact, this was essentially the accusation leveled against Paul's gospel of justification (Rom. 3:8). For justification takes place only through union with Christ, and can never be abstracted from it. *Apart from that union,* we have no share in his justification. But *in that union* in which Christ is our righteousness, he is also our sanctification (1 Cor. 1:30). We cannot be united to a half-Christ!

Thus, while justification and sanctification (holiness of

life) ought not to be confused with each other, they can never exist apart from each other, because both are the certain and invariable fruits of faith-union with Christ. Justification does not depend on sanctification, yet in union with Christ these are two sides of the same coin, so that to imagine one without the other would be to mutilate Christ. This was clearly Calvin's view:

> It is, indeed, true, that we are justified in Christ by the mercy of God alone, but it is equally true and certain, that all who are justified are called by the Lord to live worthy of their vocation. Let believers, therefore, learn to embrace Him, not only for justification, but also for sanctification, since He has been given to us for both these purposes, that they may not rend Him asunder by their own mutilated faith.[7]

This is really to say that faith never exists apart from repentance being concretely expressed in a life of new obedience to God.

But how is the justification *of sinners* possible and morally defensible?

MORAL BASIS

More specifically, the question is not merely "How does God justify?" but "How *can* God be simultaneously just and the justifier of the ungodly?"

Two elements are involved here:

1. The ungodly are forgiven. Justification in their case requires forgiveness or pardon. It is "an act of God's free grace, wherein he pardoneth all our sins."[8] Paul stresses this aspect

of justification when expounding Psalm 32:1–2 in Romans 4:7–8: "Blessed are they whose transgressions are forgiven, whose sins are covered. Blessed is the man whose sin the Lord will never count against him."

2. But there is necessarily more to justification than pardon. Pardon alone would produce only a *tabula rasa,* a clean slate. It would bring us back only to the same status as Adam had prior to the Fall. The biblical understanding of justification involves a further step. In justification, the ungodly are constituted eschatologically righteous. This is the thrust of Romans 5:19, which says that "through the obedience of the one man the many will be made righteous" (epitomizing Rom. 3:21–26). This statement grounds the confidence of Romans 8:1 that condemnation is no longer possible. For not only are we pardoned, but constituted positively, eschatologically righteous, with a righteousness that will be judgment-proof on the Last Day.

This is such a radical reversal of our natural status that we are bound to ask how God remains righteous and yet justifies the ungodly, how he can be *"just* and . . . forgive" (1 John 1:9). The answer, of course, is rooted in the work of the Christ, to whom we are united. We are justified by the redemption that is in him (Rom. 4:24).

THE WORK OF JESUS CHRIST

In Paul's teaching, the heart of the matter is located in Christ's role as the Second Man and the Last Adam (Rom. 5:12–21; 1 Cor. 15:45–49). He is an *Adam* because he was made like us in every respect, apart from sin, and is also the head of a new humanity. He is *second* because no man between Adam and Christ entered the world without sin. He is *second* also to remind us that he entered a fallen world, not the pristine world of the first Adam (Rom. 5:16). He is *last* (*eschatos*) because there is not, and need not be, any like him who follows after him, since he reverses what Adam did in his sin and also accomplishes for us what Adam failed to do.

What did the Last Adam do? He became one with us in our flesh in order to provide a righteousness in and for our humanity by (1) obeying the law of God perfectly and (2) offering himself as an atonement, life for life, death for death, substituting himself for us under the curse of God (Gal. 3:13). He kept the law on our behalf and paid the penalty for our breach of it. And—here is the genius and importance of union with Christ—since he united himself to us, what is ours by nature became his by assumption, and since by the Spirit we are united to him, what he accomplished in the Incarnation becomes ours by faith. His lifelong obedience, his sacrifice, and his "justification" are ours through what the Reformers called "the wonderful exchange" (*mirifica commutatio*).

The Gospel narratives make clear that Christ was condemned and died as the innocent substitute for sinners. Over and over again in the passion narrative, he was declared innocent (cf. Luke 23:4, 14, 15, 22, 40–41, 47). Yet he was condemned as though guilty of the twin crimes of treason against lawfully constituted authority and blasphemy against the name of God—precisely the crimes of which Adam was guilty in Eden, and of which we are guilty before God. He died in our place:

- *He* was pierced—for transgressions that were *ours*.
- *He* was crushed—for iniquities that were *ours*.
- *He* was punished—to deal with "dis-peace" that was *ours*.

81

- *He* was wounded—to heal the disease that was *ours*. (cf. Isa. 53:5)

- *He* who knew no sin was made to be *sin,* so that
- *We* who know sin might be made *righteous* in him. (cf. 2 Cor. 5:21)

Or, in specifically covenantal language:

- *Christ* became a *curse* for *sinners.*
- *Sinners* become *blessed* in *Christ.* (cf. Gal. 3:13)

So Christ grounds our pardon by bearing our guilt and punishment; he grounds our positive righteousness by providing his own perfect obedience. Consequently, our justification not only deals with past guilt, but also secures a complete, eschatological righteousness for us before God.

FAITH

Reconciliation has been accomplished in Christ. Yet, as Calvin notes, "as long as Christ remains outside of us, and we are separated from him, all that he has suffered and done for the salvation of the human race remains useless and of no value for us."[9] Hence, we find in Scripture an invariable relationship between what Christ has done and how we actively appropriate it. Again Calvin says, "We obtain this by faith."[10]

The New Testament expresses this relationship between justification and faith in various ways. We are said to be justified "through faith" (*dia pisteōs*) (Rom. 3:22), "by faith" (*ek pisteōs*) (Rom. 3:30), and "by faith" (*pistei*) (Rom. 3:28). But we are never said to be justified "on account of faith" (*kata pistin*), that is, on the basis of faith itself as the ground of justification. Faith is, in the technical terminology of the theologians, the instrumental cause, not the material cause of justification. Thus, according to the Westminster Confession, "Faith, thus receiving and resting on Christ and His righteousness, is the alone instrument of justification."[11]

Paul powerfully underlines this in Romans 4:1ff., where he demonstrates that Abraham's justification came not through works (4:1–8), nor by the instrument of sacramental administration (4:9–12), nor by performance of the law (4:13–15), but by faith. He trusted in the God who promised him a seed that would be a blessing to the nations (Gen. 12:2–3). Again, as Christ is the proper object of our faith, so Christ (as the promised seed) was the resting place of his trust and commitment.

But this raises an important question. Why should faith be the appropriating instrument in justification? At one level, the answer is that since our justification is in Christ, it can be ours only through a personal fellowship with him; and faith introduces us to such fellowship, since we put our faith "into" (*eis*) Christ and are thus united to him.

But at another level, the answer is that faith is the appropriate instrument of justification because in its very nature faith is active in receiving Christ, but noncontributory (in that sense "passive" or, perhaps better, "receptive") in relation to the justification we receive. It has no constructive energy; it is complete reliance on another. It is Christ-directed, not self-directed, and Christ-reliant, not self-reliant. It involves the abandoning, not the congratulating, of self.

Consequently, as Paul notes in Romans 3:27, boasting "is excluded." His answer to the question "On what principle?"

83

is illuminating. It is not on the principle of law or works. That is true because we do not live up to the demands of the law. But it is true at another level also. The principle of law or works theoretically leaves room for human achievement, and therefore for boasting. But, Paul says, boasting is excluded *on the principle of faith*. Why? By definition, faith excludes even the possibility of boasting. The "promise [of justification] comes by faith, so that it may be by grace" (Rom. 4:16). "By faith" actually implies "by grace," because of the very nature of faith as a receptor rather than a contributor. Faith draws everything from Christ and contributes nothing to him. *Faith* is simply a shorthand description of abandoning oneself trustingly to Christ, whom God has made our righteousness. Therefore, says Paul, "Let him who boasts boast in the Lord" (1 Cor. 1:30–31).

Faith thus takes its character and power from its object, not from itself.

These were the biblical considerations that lay behind the Reformation's doctrine of faith, and which enabled the Reformers to pinpoint with new clarity just exactly what was involved in faith in Christ.

THE REFORMATION DOCTRINE OF FAITH

The Reformers' doctrine of faith was worked out against the specific background of the medieval order of salvation. The Roman teaching operated with two important distinctions in relation to faith:

1. A distinction between *fides implicita* and *fides explicita*. The former was "implicit faith" in the teaching given by the church, on the basis of the teaching office of the church.

2. But the medieval theologians and the Church of Rome developed a further distinction, between *fides informis* and *fides formata (charitate),* i.e., "unformed faith" and "formed faith," or faith that is formed by and issued in love. Unformed faith could be evoked by a fear of divine justice that drove the individual to hope in Christ and to that initial love expressed in contrition. If this contrition was suffused with perfect love and desire for the Sacrament, then justification took place. But if that sorrow (*contritio*) was imperfect (i.e., *attritio*), then justification would be received only through the sacrament of penance, with its climax in absolution. In the earlier institution of penance, satisfaction for sin preceded absolution. In the later sacrament of penance, satisfaction followed absolution and had to do with the mitigation of temporal penalties.

It is not difficult to see what deeply disturbed the Reformers about this teaching. Justification became the goal to which the individual moves, not the foundation on which the whole Christian life is lived. It was placed too much in the "not yet," whereas in the gospel it belongs to the "already" of the Christian's life.

It was also at root semi-Pelagian. It was said that we are saved by grace. In fact, Roman theology spoke much about "grace." But that grace was so intimately related to our own works of sanctification that its nature was distorted and its true role was obscured. This, in turn, affected the role of faith and the significance of Christ.[12] Hence, the *sola* watchwords of the Reformation were intended to spell out the sheer graciousness and unmerited character of grace: *sola fide, sola gratia, sola Scriptura,* and *solo Christo* all related to this teaching.

When we understand this background, we realize that while Rome always taught that salvation was never without grace, it denied that it was by grace alone and faith alone. It thus essentially dis-graced grace. Against that background, it is not difficult to understand the sheer joy of the Reformation's rediscovery of the biblical teaching on faith alone.

For the Reformers, faith has three dimensions: *notitia* (or *cognitio*), *assensus,* and *fiducia*. It involves knowledge of God's revelation in general and specifically of his revelation in Jesus Christ.[13] It includes assent to biblical revelation (*sola Scriptura*). And such assent is based on and compelled by the truth of the gospel. It is "forced" upon us, irresistibly, by the truth of the gospel. In common with every other kind of faith, it is always "forced consent." As Murray writes,

> Faith is *forced* consent. That is to say, when evidence is judged by the mind to be sufficient, the state of mind we call "faith" is the inevitable precipitate. It is not something we can resist or in respect of which we may suspend judgment. In such a case faith is compelled. It is demanded, it is commanded. For whenever the reasons are apprehended or judged sufficient, will we, nill we, faith or belief is induced. Will to the contrary, desire to the contrary, overwhelming interest to the contrary, cannot make us believe the opposite of our judgment with respect to the evidence.[14]

But, supremely, faith is *fiducia*—personal trust in Christ, without the mediation of priest and sacrament (*solo Christo*). The believing man trusts directly in Christ. Faith is thus "a heart trust which the Holy Ghost works in me by the Gospel."[15] Consequently, for the Reformers, faith implies a joyful assurance of salvation in Christ, a "sure and certain knowledge of God's benevolence towards us,"[16] as Calvin put it. The believer is not left in darkness, doubt, and anxiety about his salvation.

Such an exposition of faith emphasizes in biblical fashion the human responsibility involved in believing and at the same time completely preserves the grace of God in the way of salvation. *Cognitio* arises out of the grace of revelation, *assensus* is evoked by the authority of the gospel, and *fiducia* is ours, not because of anything in us, but only because of the utter trustworthiness of our Savior Jesus Christ!

THE CHARACTER OF FAITH

By way of summary, several things should be emphasized about justifying faith:

1. *Faith contributes no merit.* It is the nature of faith, indeed its very genius, that by it we actively receive justification in Christ without contributing to it. After all, faith is trust in another. It is the antithesis of all self-contribution or self-trust. The promise of salvation is made to faith. Why? So that it might be by grace and be guaranteed to believers (Rom. 4:16). Faith engages grace without meriting it in any way. B. B. Warfield puts it this way:

> The *saving power* of faith resides thus not in itself, but in the Almighty Saviour on whom it rests. . . . It is not faith that saves, but faith in Jesus Christ. . . . It is not, strictly speaking, even faith in Christ that saves, but Christ that saves through faith. The saving power resides exclusively, not in the act of faith or the attitude of faith or the nature of faith, but in the object of faith. . . . We could not more radically misconceive it than by transferring to faith even the smallest fraction of that saving energy which is attributed in the Scriptures wholly to Christ himself.[17]

We are saved by Christ as we believe. There is total engagement of the believer, yet at the same time grace is not compromised.

2. *Faith is a gift of God.* Philippians 1:29 provides an important perspective here: "It has been granted to you on behalf of Christ not only to believe on him, but also to suffer for him." Suffering is a gift of grace in Christian experience. So is faith.

This parallel between faith and suffering helps to safeguard us from a misunderstanding of faith as a gift. The gift of suffering is not a commodity we receive as a *fait accompli.* We suffer in the sovereign purposes of God. But it is *we*—not God—who experience the suffering. In the same way, in his grace God gives us faith, but it is exercised by us, not by him. We—not God—are the ones who believe!

Thus, even if the classic text of Ephesians 2:8—"It is by grace you have been saved, through faith—and this not from yourselves, it is the gift of God"—may carry a broader interpretation,[18] Paul confirms that faith is a divine gift later in Ephesians 6:23 when he prays for "faith from God the Father and the Lord Jesus Christ." Whatever comes from God is given in grace. Yet, as Otto Weber well puts it, "Faith, according to the biblical understanding does not consist of man's being set aside, but of his being involved to the uttermost."[19]

3. *Faith is capable of degrees.* The New Testament speaks of faith in various ways: little faith (Matt. 14:31), great faith (Matt. 15:28), unfeigned faith (2 Tim. 1:5), and strong faith (Rom. 4:20). Yet the least faith saves, and ultimately also overcomes (1 John 5:4), because it gives us a great Savior.

These different "degrees" of faith have in view the extent to which we respond to God in a manner commensurate with the greatness and trustworthiness of his promise. Weak faith focuses on immediate circumstances; by contrast, great or strong faith is trust that responds in a way consistent with the greatness of its object. Thus, Abraham grew strong in faith as he refused to allow himself to be influenced by the circumstances of Sarah's barrenness and his own age, and instead allowed his life to be determined by the promise of God, and gave glory to him (Rom. 4:20).

FAITH AND GOOD WORKS

Salvation, including justification, Paul argues, is by faith, not by works. Yet at first sight there is a paradox here. For the New Testament indicates that we will be judged according to our works: "We must all appear before the judgment seat of Christ, that each one may receive what is due him for the things done while in the body, whether good or bad" (2 Cor. 5:10). The works of teachers of the gospel are tested by fire (1 Cor. 3:12–13). Other statements, such as Ephesians 6:8 ("The Lord will reward everyone for whatever good he does"), Colossians 3:24–25 ("You will receive an inheritance from the Lord as a reward. . . . Anyone who does wrong will be repaid for his wrong, and there is no favoritism"), and 1 Peter 1:17 (God "judges each man's work impartially"), further emphasize the importance of works with respect to divine judgment on our lives.

The clue to interpreting these statements is well expressed by Philip Hughes:

It is important to see that the purpose of this tribunal is not positively penal, but properly retributive, involving the disclosure not only of what has been worthless, but also of what has been good and valuable in this life. The judgment pronounced is not a declaration of doom, but *an assessment of worth,* with the assignment of rewards to those who because of their faithfulness deserve them.[20]

The point is that the reality of future judgment according to works in no sense compromises the finality of present justification by faith, to which works make no contribution, but are rather its fruit.

JAMES: A LETTER OF STRAW?

But when we turn to James 2:14–26, the question arises whether the New Testament's teaching is quite so straightforward. That issue is most pointedly raised by the stark nature of James's conclusion: "You see that a person is justified by what he does and not by faith alone" (James 2:24). Is it any wonder that the Luther of *sola fide* thought of the letter of James as an epistle of straw?

It may help here if we notice two things:

THE CONTRAST EXPOUNDED BY JAMES

Part of the complexity of James's argument derives from the fact that he is contrasting two different persons, both of whom profess to be genuine believers. We may call them "Faith A" and "Faith B." Each believes his faith is authentic. Hence, James speaks of both as having "faith." But he will eventually demonstrate that Faith A is not really saving faith; indeed, it is not faith at all.

Faith A is:
>   Faith without deeds (vv. 14, 18, 20, 26)
>   Faith in contrast to deeds (v. 18)
>   Faith in itself, i.e., unaccompanied by action (v. 17)
>   Faith alone, i.e., isolated from deeds (v. 24)

Faith B is:
>   Faith shown by what it does (v. 18)
>   Faith accompanied by actions (v. 22)
>   Faith consummated by actions (v. 23)

James asks whether the former, Faith A, can save (v. 14). Both the logic of his argument and the grammatical form of his question indicate that he expects a negative answer. Why? Because Faith A does not work.

On what basis does he reach this conclusion? Saving or justifying faith always expresses itself in good works. Unless professed faith is working faith, it is not saving faith and therefore cannot be true faith. To borrow Paul's language, true faith, saving faith, always works by love (cf. Gal. 5:6).

James's teaching has often been seen as a potential embarrassment to Paul's gospel, and consequently harmonization has often driven its interpretation. But the proper interpretation of James's words should not be formulated along a Paul-James axis, for example, by suggesting that James is using either or both of the terms *faith* and *justify* in different senses from Paul. In fact, Paul is not his conversation partner here; moral indifference is.

In fact, James himself is using *faith* in two quite different senses. He is also teaching that the faith by which a person is considered righteous (James 2:23) will always be fulfilled by that person acting in a righteous manner. He or she is therefore quite properly considered to be righteous.

THE CONCLUSION DRAWN BY JAMES

When James draws his conclusion—"You see that a person is justified by what he does and not by faith alone" (v. 24)—his logic is shaped by the Abraham narrative. Earlier (in v. 23), James has cited Genesis 15:6, which rests justification instrumentally in faith, having already stated that Abraham was "considered righteous for what he did when he offered his son Isaac on the altar" (2:21). These two statements he sees as complementary, not contradictory. Abraham was justified by faith and was also "justified" (in the sense of being considered righteous, i.e., rightly related to God in his covenant) for what he did. He was thus later counted righteous for the simple reason that he was righteous—not sinless, but faithful to his covenant Lord.

James's teaching here in essence is that the man who is righteous by faith will be recognized and counted as righteous through his deeds, just as Abraham was.

The key, then, is verse 18: What a man does is the touchstone of faith. So, true faith, which alone justifies, is expressed by what a man does, not by what he presumes. The man who lives faithfully is the justified man (although he is not justified by living faithfully). Deedless faith cannot save, not because works are the ground of justification, but because the lack of works is the evidence of the absence of real faith.

James's basic point is that the faith alone by which we are justified is not an abstraction. It unites us to Christ as our righteousness and simultaneously as our sanctification. Expressed otherwise, James teaches that if he who professes faith is not also one whose faith expresses itself in practical works, then he does not believe with a faith that receives justification, and therefore does not believe truly. The one who genuinely believes is united to Christ, in the power of his new life, and such a one is also sanctified in Christ and works for his glory. As John Murray puts it, "Faith alone justifies but a justified person with faith alone would be a monstrosity which never exists in the kingdom of grace."[21] Or, as Calvin says,

> We confess with Paul that no other faith justifies but faith working through love. But it does not take its power to justify from that working of love. Indeed it justifies in no other way but in that it leads us into fellowship with the righteousness of Christ.[22]

This is also what the Westminster Confession is at pains to emphasize:

> Faith . . . is the alone instrument of justification: yet is it not alone in the person justified, but is ever accompanied with all other saving graces, and is no dead faith, but worketh by love.[23]

Such faith, said Luther, is always "a busy little thing." That is why faith alone, *sola fide,* is never lonely!

5

DEFINITE ATONEMENT

O. PALMER ROBERTSON

Death is a commonplace thing. As a matter of fact, there have been just as many deaths on the face of the earth as there have been billions of people who have lived. Considering all the deaths that have occurred, what can one death be expected to accomplish?

Some deaths do accomplish something. In warfare, one soldier may die for another. He may heroically throw himself on a grenade, giving up his life to shield the lives of others. In a sense, the death of every soldier fighting for his country accomplishes something.

In history, certain deaths have accomplished significant things. On June 28, 1914, Archduke Franz Ferdinand, heir to the throne of Austria-Hungary, was visiting Sarajevo in Bosnia. A bomb was thrown at his car. The archduke was unhurt, though some of the members of his entourage had to be taken to the hospital. Later that day, the archduke directed his driver to take him by the hospital where his wounded companions were being treated. The driver took a wrong turn, realized what he had done, and stopped the car to put it in reverse. Just at that moment, a startled nineteen-year-old aspiring assassin named Gavrilo Princip stepped forward, pulled out his pistol, and shot the archduke and his wife dead.

WHAT CAN ONE DEATH ACCOMPLISH?

This death ignited the First World War. The death of this one man led to the death of millions. The flower of Europe's youth spent years in mud-soaked trenches. This one man's death led to the reordering of the political world, which eventually led to the rise of Adolf Hitler and World War II.

A certain other death in history accomplished much more. It secured universal peace rather than world war. This other death accomplished the reconciliation of men with God, and men with men. Untold millions have passed from death to life because of the death of the one man Jesus Christ. The entire created universe has been reordered by this one man's death. So consider the death of Jesus Christ and what it accomplished.

GOD'S ETERNAL PURPOSES

The death of Jesus Christ accomplished the realization of God's eternal purposes. The covenant Lord, as revealed in creation and the Scriptures, is great, greater than all other supposed gods (Ps. 135:5). He does whatever he pleases, both in heaven and on earth (Ps. 135:6). A vital part of his eternal purpose is the salvation of sinners. As a consequence, a great number from every tribe, kindred, language, and nation have been chosen for eternal salvation. They have been "predestined according to the plan of him who works out everything in conformity with the purpose of his will" (Eph. 1:11).

This purpose to save a great multitude from among the whole of humanity has been clearly made known by God. But in realizing that purpose, God in his integrity had to remain true to his own righteousness and justice, even as he manifested his love and mercy. Once he had determined to save a multitude of sinners, a proper righteousness had to be provided on their behalf. The just punishment that these people deserved for their sins had to be suffered by someone.

The perfect life and the atoning death of Jesus Christ accomplished this righteousness. God presented his Son as a sacrifice to suffer the just punishment that sin deserves. The Father offered up the Son so that he might be just, even while declaring guilty sinners to be righteous and without blame. The purpose of God in providing a way of redemption from the consequences of sin came to realization through the death of his Son. As a consequence of his death, millions of people have been delivered from the punishment they deserve.

Is the eternal purpose of God being realized in your own personal salvation? Are you numbered among that great host of people for whom Christ died? Did his death pay the penalty that is due to you for your sin? Do you today repudiate your sinful ways and cry out for the mercy of God that is found in the death of Jesus Christ? Have you put your trust for the forgiveness of your sins completely in the sacrifice of the Son of God? If you have saving faith in Christ today, you can know that you personally were a part of the eternal plan of God for the salvation of sinners, and that Jesus Christ had you in mind when he suffered the punishment due to sin.

How amazing! The eternal purpose of almighty God for the salvation of sinners was realized in the one death of the one man Jesus Christ. His death has brought to fulfillment the plan of God made ages ago in eternity past.

ACTUAL REDEMPTION

The nature of the Atonement—the death of Jesus—underscores the actual accomplishment of redemption. The death of Jesus Christ brought about the realization of the eternal purposes of God. Consider still further what the death of Jesus accomplished.

1. *The death of Jesus Christ was a priestly sacrifice for sinners.* Under the provisions of the old covenant, the high priest of Israel never offered his sacrifices for people indiscriminately. The priestly sacrifices were always offered for specific sinners. The high priest presented his sacrifice for a great multitude, but always for a specific multitude. On his shoulders and on his chest, the high priest bore the names of the tribes of Israel, engraved on precious stones. He was to "bear the names on his shoulders as a memorial before the LORD" (Ex. 28:12). As a further indication of the people for whom he offered sacrifices, he was to "bear the names of the sons of Israel over his heart on the breastpiece . . . as a continuing memorial before the LORD" (Ex. 28:29). It was specifically for these people that the high priest offered his atoning sacrifice.

In a similar way, the sacrifice of Jesus Christ, our high priest, was offered for the sins of a great multitude, but a multitude of specific people. His sacrifice was offered for a particular people taken from all the nations of the world. John 17 records the High Priestly Prayer of Christ. Just a few hours before his death, Jesus offered his sacrifice of intercessory prayer. Note the repeated emphasis in this prayer on the specific objects of Christ's intercession:

> You granted [me] authority over all people that [I] might give eternal life to all those you have given [me]. (v. 2)

> I have revealed you to those whom you gave me out of the world. (v. 6)

> They [the ones you have given me] believed that you sent me. (v. 8)

> I pray for them; I am not praying for the world, but for those you have given me. (v. 9)

Jesus' priestly work of prayer on the night before his death was directly connected to his priestly work of sacrifice. He presented his life as a sacrifice for the same people for whom he had been praying. This priestly work of prayer and sacrifice actually accomplished salvation for his people, the very ones the Father had given him. The whole point of the substitutionary sacrifice of Christ was that he was giving his life in the place of those who had been given to him by the Father.

So what did the priestly prayer and sacrifice of Christ achieve? Did it make possible the salvation of all sinners? Or was his life offered in actual substitution for each and every one of those who had been given to him by the Father?

The repeated statements of the Lord on the night before he presented himself as a sacrifice make the answer to this question quite evident. The death of Jesus Christ actually accomplished the salvation of all those whom the Father had given to him. If you today are a believer in Christ, it is because he had your name on his heart as he offered himself in prayer and sacrifice to the Father. By his priestly sacrifice, he actually accomplished salvation for all those whom the Father had given him.

2. *The death of Christ was a propitiation, removing the wrath of God from sinners.* When the publican in Jesus' parable came to the temple to pray, he would not even lift his eyes to heaven. He smote his breast and cried out, "God, have mercy on [*or,* be propitiated toward] me, a sinner" (Luke 18:13). He saw himself, and rightly so, as the object of the wrath of God. For God's righteous wrath has been revealed from heaven against all ungodliness and unrighteousness of men (Rom. 1:18). Even when people are blind to the fact, the righteous wrath of God repeatedly manifests itself toward sinful mankind.

While Jesus Christ hung on the cross, he received the wrath of God for sin. "My God, my God, why have you forsaken me?" was his cry (Matt. 27:46). Sin received the full fury of the holy God at the cross of Christ.

But whose sin received the just judgment of God's righteous wrath at that crucial moment? Clearly it was not Jesus' own sin, for "he committed no sin, and no deceit was found in his mouth" (1 Peter 2:22). Instead, Jesus absorbed in himself the full wrath of God for a great multitude of sinners from every tribe, kindred, nation, and people. In the agonies of his death, he absorbed in himself the full wrath of God for this great multitude of sinners. As a consequence of Christ's propitiatory death, God was perfectly at peace with these sinners.

But which sinners? Did Christ propitiate the wrath of God for each and every person in the world? Did he remove the wrath of God from every human being by his death? If his death had this effect, then every human being who has ever lived must be saved forever from the wrath of God. For God is just, and if his wrath has been expended on his Son for every human being, he would not be just in pouring out his wrath once more on those for whom Christ died.

Jesus himself answers the question concerning the people for whom he died. "I am the good shepherd. The good shepherd lays down his life for the sheep," he said (John 10:11). "I know my sheep. . . . I lay down my life for the sheep. . . . I have other sheep" (John 10:14–16). Does not the shepherd know his sheep? Yes, he knows his sheep by name. He gives his life for the sheep that he knows by name. He calls these sheep by name, they hear his voice, and he gives them eternal life.

The death of Jesus Christ was perfectly effective in absorbing the wrath of God for his sheep. From eternity past he has known them by name. The propitiatory nature of his death in effectively removing the wrath of God from sinners means that his life was not offered indiscriminately. Instead, his death removed the wrath of God forever from all those whom the Father had given him.

Are you like the publican who sensed the wrath of God hovering over his head? Then cry out like the publican. Humbly plead with the Lord to remove his wrath from you. The publican left the temple a justified man on that very day (Luke 18:14). The fact that he humbled himself indicates that he was one of those people given to the Son by the Father. If you will humble yourself and cry out for the mercy of God toward sinners as it is found in Jesus Christ, you can be like the publican. You can be declared righteous before the tribunal of God despite your sin, and you can rest assured that the death of Jesus has removed the wrath of God from you once and for all.

3. *In his death, Jesus redeemed sinners by paying the price for their sin and thereby purchasing them for himself.* Each sin that each human being commits creates a debt to God the Creator. Because the sinner cannot repay that debt, God's justice requires that the sinner suffer the just punishment for his sin, which is death. Jesus Christ took upon himself the debt to God's justice owed by sinners. By his death, he paid their debt, and so redeemed those sinners, purchasing them for himself.

But which sinners have been redeemed? Who has been purchased by the death of Christ? If Jesus paid the debt for all sin, then all sinners have been redeemed and purchased by him. As a consequence, the whole of humanity would be eternally saved. No further payment for sin would be required, for God is just and would not demand a double payment for any person's sin.

Suppose you were a young man just married, and had to borrow money to get set up in a home. Suppose your kind father paid your entire debt to the bank. What would you think if the banker then demanded that you pay the debt a second time? It would not be allowed. Justice would not permit it.

Similarly, God will not demand a double payment for sin, once by his Son and once by the sinner. By his death, Jesus paid the full price for the redemption of his people. He bought his church with his own blood. As the apostle Paul admonishes the elders of the church at Ephesus, "Be shepherds of the church of God, which he bought with his own blood" (Acts 20:28). The transaction has been completed. The price has been paid. The church has been redeemed from all her sins. It is not that Jesus simply made salvation possible for all people; instead, he actually accomplished salvation for his church.

Think for a moment about your sins—all of them. Every sin you have committed in thought, word, or deed has indebted you to the justice of God. It may not be the most pleasant exercise, but think specifically of one of the worst sins you have ever committed. Perhaps you will remember a sin you committed in the folly of your youth. On the other hand, you may recall a sin of your more mature years, when you should have known better.

Although you may not have thought about it, one of the worst sins you have ever committed is the sin of unbelief! All those days you lived without believing in Jesus Christ were sinful days. You were insulting the Son of God by not trusting in him. Those sins of unbelief made you a debtor to God.

Did Christ die to pay for your sins of unbelief? If you are today a believer in Christ, the answer is yes. His death was completely effective in paying off the debt for all your sins of unbelief. But if you never turn to him, never believe in him, be sure of this fact: he did not die for your sins of unbelief. He did not die for the unbelief of all people. He died only for the sins of unbelief committed by the people who would eventually come to believe in him. These are the sheep that Christ purchased with his own blood.

If you today are unrepentant for your unbelief, be assured of this fact. You cannot claim that Christ died for your sins. He did not pour out his lifeblood for the sins of unbelief committed by all people. Turn now. Weep for the years that you have insulted the sacrifice of the Son of God. Cast your entire hope on the one who gave himself for sinners just like you. Then you can be assured that you will find full and free forgiveness for all your sins against him.

4. *The death of Jesus has effected an abiding reconciliation between an offended God and an offending sinner.* When there is a need for reconciliation, two people are at enmity with one an-

other. They need to be at peace, but they are at war. In the Bible, it is not merely that sinners are at war with God; he is also at war with sinners (Rom. 5:10). He is the mighty warrior who goes forth against all his enemies. After a period of patience, he brings sudden destruction on his enemies.

In the death of Jesus Christ, it is not in the first place the sinner's enmity against God that comes to an end. Instead, it is God's enmity against sinners that is removed. Paul makes this point plain in his letter to the Romans. "While we were still sinners, Christ died for us" (Rom. 5:8). Even while the sinner remains at war against God, the death of Christ effects a reconciliation (Rom. 5:10). God demonstrates his own love for us in this way: while our enmity still continued, God was reconciled to us by the death of his Son.

But who more precisely are the "we" with whom God has been reconciled? Has Christ actually removed God's wrath toward all people by his death? Has the whole of humanity been reconciled to God? Scripture makes it plain that all sinners have not been reconciled to God. Many will appear at the Last Day at God's left hand, and will depart into the everlasting fire prepared for the devil and his angels (Matt. 25:41–46).

But God, through the death of Christ, has been reconciled to a great multitude from every tribe, kindred, nation, and people. If you in your own spirit have been reconciled to him, it is because he was first reconciled to you. If you love him, it is because he first loved you (1 John 4:19). If you have died to your old hostility against God and his ways, it is because God was first reconciled to you in the death of his Son.

This double reconciliation is a glorious reality for each and every person who is in Christ. As the apostle says, "Christ's love compels us, because we are convinced that one died for all, and therefore all died" (2 Cor. 5:14). At first reading, it might appear that this statement affirms that Christ's death was effective for all people. But it must be noted that in this statement "all" those for whom Christ died are "all" those who themselves have died. Who then are the "all" who have died? This dying by all is obviously not referring to physical death, since many people have not yet died in this sense. Instead, this dying refers to a dying to self, as the next verse explains: "He died for all, that those who live should no longer live for themselves but for him who died for them, and was raised again" (v. 15). In this verse, the expression "those who . . . no longer live for themselves" clearly does not refer to all human beings, but to all those who have been made alive in Christ. These are therefore the "all" for whom he died, that is, all those who are in him.

So, as Paul continues, God was in Christ "reconciling the world to himself" (2 Cor. 5:19). This reconciliation of "the world" does not refer to each and every person in the world, but to the world considered from the perspective of its alienation from God, and having no other way of reconciliation except that which God himself has chosen to provide in Christ.

In calling forth a proper response to God's accomplished reconciliation from all who are by God's grace "in Christ," the apostle admonishes, "Be reconciled to God" (2 Cor. 5:20). God has put aside his enmity in the sacrifice of his Son for all who are "in Christ"; now these people are urged to put aside their enmity by embracing for themselves the reconciliation to God that is found in Christ.

So the death of Jesus Christ has not merely opened the door to the possibility of a reconciliation of alienated sinners to God. Instead, God is already reconciled to sinners who are in Christ, and these sinners are urged to set aside their alienation toward God, so that they may be reconciled to him.

So what has one death, the death of Jesus Christ, accomplished? This death has provided a sufficient priestly sacrifice. It has accomplished an effective propitiation by the removal of the wrath of God. It has provided a full redemption by the purchase of a people. It has accomplished a genuine reconciliation by the removal of God's enmity toward all who are in Christ. These accomplishments are not hypothetical possibilities, but actual realities directed specifically toward all those on whom God has set his purposeful love before the foundation of the world.

But that's not all that Christ's death accomplished. His death did not only fulfill the eternal purpose of God and make atonement for a great multitude of sinners from every tribe, kindred, nation, and people. One further accomplishment must be noted.

BOTH THE END AND THE MEANS OF REDEMPTION

The death of Jesus was effective in purchasing not only the end of our redemption, but also the means to that end.

Suppose some gracious person pays for you to fly to Europe for a vacation. When that person makes his payment, he purchases more than the trip itself. He also purchases the airline ticket that will get you on the plane. If you should arrive at the airline counter and proudly announce, "Someone has paid for me to fly to Europe," the agent will invariably respond, "Where's your ticket?" No ticket, no flight.

So Jesus Christ in his death not only paid for your transfer from the kingdom of darkness and death into the kingdom of light and life. By his death, he also purchased the "ticket" that enables you to make the transition.

What is that ticket? It is your faith in the completed work of Christ. Only true faith in Christ, together with the accompanying grace of repentance, can make the atonement of Christ effective in its application to you.

I once heard a preacher declare that Jesus' death might not have saved anyone. In fact, said he, when Jesus died, he didn't know whether anyone would believe in him. He could only hope that his death would not be in vain.

Nonsense! Jesus Christ, the great high priest, knew exactly which people he was dying for. Just as the high priest of Israel bore the names of the tribes of Israel on his forehead and his chest, so Jesus bore the names of his people in his heart at the time of his death. He who had called the stars by name at creation now recalled the names of each and every one of God's elect at the moment when he offered himself for their redemption. If you are a believer in Christ today, consider this awesome fact. Jesus remembered your name before the Father when he died on the cross.

To insure your complete salvation, Jesus purchased by his death not only your redemption, but also the faith by which you would receive that redemption. Christ earned faith and spiritual grace for those for whom he died. If follows, then, that those who have no faith are not those for whom he died.

As a corollary to this statement, it may be affirmed that all those who believe in Christ are proved to be those for whom he died. For only by the purchase price of Christ's death has anyone ever come to believe in him. Never think you are smarter or more pious than others because you believe. Only at the awful price of Christ's blood was your faith purchased. Scripture says it over and over in many different ways. Faith is God's gift to you, purchased by Christ:

> It has been granted to you on behalf of Christ . . . to believe on him. (Phil. 1:29)

God exalted him . . . that he might give repentance . . . to Israel. (Acts 5:31)

All that the Father gives me will come to me [that is, believe in me]. (John 6:37)

My sheep listen to my voice [that is, believe in me]. (John 10:27)

(Note the previous statement of Jesus, spoken to the Jews: "You do not believe because you are not my sheep" (John 10:26). Although it would be true, Jesus does not say the reverse: "You are not my sheep because you do not believe.")

I have other sheep. . . . They too will listen to my voice [that is, believe in me]. (John 10:16)

All who were appointed for eternal life believed. (Acts 13:48)

The Lord opened [Lydia's] heart to respond to Paul's message. (Acts 16:14)

[Apollos] was a great help to those who by grace had believed. (Acts 18:27)

The classic words found in Ephesians 2:8–9 underscore this same principle: "For by grace you have been saved through faith, and that not of yourselves; it is the gift of God, not of works, lest anyone should boast" (Eph. 2:8–9 NKJV). But is this "faith" to be regarded as the contribution that the sinner finally makes to his own salvation? Or does this passage intend to affirm that even faith is a part of God's gift in salvation?

A careful analysis of the pronouns of the passage answers

this question quite precisely. The words "grace" and "faith" are both feminine, while the participle "you have been saved" is masculine. But the "it" that is "the gift of God" is neuter, which means that it cannot refer specifically to "grace," "faith," or "salvation." If "it" did refer back to "grace," "faith," or "salvation," then it might be concluded that one or more of these things is not included in the gift of God. But as the text reads, "it" embraces all these elements. "Grace" is a gift, "faith" is a gift, and "salvation" is a gift. Our salvation was achieved by Christ's death, and our faith was purchased by his blood.

So the atoning death of Christ was completely effective. His death purchased not only reconciliation to God, but also the means necessary for receiving the blessings of that reconciliation.

Did Christ make that purchase for all men? Did he die equally for all? If so, all would believe, and all would be saved. He would have died to pay the price for the unbelief of all and given his life to purchase faith for all.

Did Christ make the purchase for his people, for the undeserving sinners given to him by the Father? Indeed he did. For that reason, the death of the one man Jesus Christ accomplished a wondrous thing. By his death, he accomplished full redemption for a great multitude from every tribe, kindred, nation, and people.

CONCLUSION

See what the death of one man can accomplish! How glorious is the completed redemption purchased by Christ. So how should you respond?

First, whosoever will, let him come! If you come, then certainly your sins will have been paid for by him, and so you shall be saved. Christ died for all who will come, and all for whom he died will come. If you desire a complete and completed salvation today, then come to Jesus Christ.

Second, be humbled if you do believe. You did not generate your faith of yourself. Your faith was purchased at infinite cost to Christ, by his sufferings on the cross. Why then should you have any sense of pride?

Third, remain unshaken in your assurance of salvation. If you had generated your own faith, or had earned your own acceptance before God, you might one day lose your faith. But if your faith arose in your heart because of the price paid by Christ, you may be sure that it will always remain with you. Your salvation is rooted in the undeserved election of God, determined in eternity past. Therefore, it can never be lost.

Fourth, go forth with the gospel! If the atoning death of Christ will prove to be effective for the salvation of a great multitude that no man can number, if their faith in him has already been purchased by his death, then go! Be assured that some will believe. He has other sheep that are not of his Jewish fold. They will hear his voice. Christ did not merely make salvation possible for all, which could result in the salvation of none. He paid the price for many. So go! Remember the words of assurance given to the apostle Paul: "I have many people in this city" (Acts 18:9–10). Remember the apostle's response in his last inspired letter: "I endure everything for the sake of the elect, that they too may obtain the salvation that is in Christ Jesus, with eternal glory" (2 Tim. 2:10).

Fifth, give all glory to God. Whether people believe or not, God will be glorified. Some will believe. Many will not believe. But God will be glorified by the work accomplished by the death of his Son.

6

SOLA GRATIA

MICHAEL S. HORTON

Already laureled in his native land and university, Oxford don Thomas Bradwardine experienced what he described as a conversion. Early on in his studies, "the school of Pelagius seemed to me nearest the truth. . . . What I heard day in and day out was that we are masters of our own free acts, that ours is the choice to act well or badly, to have virtues or sins and much more along this line." And "every time I listened to the Epistle reading in church and heard how Paul magnified grace and belittled free will—as is the case in Romans 9, 'It is obviously not a question of human will and effort, but of divine mercy,' and its many parallels— grace displeased me, ungrateful as I was." It was when he began to study this ninth chapter of Paul's letter to the Romans, says Bradwardine, that "the text mentioned came to me as a beam of grace and, captured by a vision of the truth, it seemed I saw from afar how the grace of God precedes all good works. . . . That is why I express my gratitude to him who has given me this grace as a free gift."[1] As a result of this shift, Bradwardine wrote a provocative little book, *De causa Dei, contra Pelagium* (The Case of God against the New Pelagians). Named after a fourth-century British monk who was irritated by the dominance of Augustine's grace-oriented theology, Pelagianism held that human beings achieve salvation by their own efforts.

This broadside from the pen of Thomas Bradwardine against what he regarded as the creeping moralism of his day was not written recently, however. Nor was it written by a cranky "paleo-Calvinist," as many today would put it. It was the Oxford of the fourteenth century, and Bradwardine was the archbishop of Canterbury. Less than two centuries later, Martin Luther and John Calvin could not help but see their battle in the similar terms of Jesus versus the Pharisees, Paul versus the Judaizers, and Augustine versus Pelagius. The Reformers recognized that Pelagianism was the practical, working theology of their day, although it remained officially condemned.

This heresy rested on a denial of original sin and an emphasis on an autonomous and neutral free will. Pelagius and his supporters concluded that the power of sin and divine judgment for it had their cause in individual choice rather than inborn sinfulness. Human beings become sinners by following Adam's poor example, and they become holy by following Christ's good example. Understandably, then, "What has Jesus done?" became a subservient question to "What would Jesus do?" The debate over Pelagianism consumed the energies of the church throughout the late fourth and early fifth centuries, but as one looks across the horizon of time and place, it seems merely one name for a heresy that has taken many forms.

With the Enlightenment came fresh charges of Pelagianism as moderns championed ethics over redemption, raised confidence in human achievement, reason, and social perfection, and left room for God only as a creator-lawgiver to keep moral progress moving along. Immanuel Kant, who most embodied these beliefs, openly embraced Pelagianism, regarding Jesus Christ as little more than an example for moral duty. Autonomy (self-rule), resting on the notion of an absolute free will, worked itself out into every discipline, including theology, until no doctrine of supernatural Christianity was left unchallenged. But what was one to put in its place? Nietzsche famously pointed up that question, concluding that when Christian morality is severed from Christian theology, neither can remain. This leaves an emptiness that can ultimately be filled only by the "madman"—an insight that the twentieth century amply validated.

This historical vignette underscores the perennial attraction of, and antidote for, Pelagianism in every age. Our purpose here is to think out loud concerning this temptation and its effects in our churches—yes, *ours,* even if they wear the labels "Reformed" and "Presbyterian" and endeavor to be such. At the outset, it should be said that the purpose here is not to vilify anyone or pinpoint blame. In fact, this article suggests that the "new Pelagianism" of our day often coexists among churches and individuals thoroughly opposed to it in theory. That is due partly to the fact that this new Pelagianism is practically indistinguishable from modernity itself. In fact, one could say that modernity is a secularized Pelagianism.

In this paradigm, the human being is no longer regarded

as in every way dependent upon, or even answerable to, a Creator, but is treated as a self-sufficient creator in his or her own right, constructing reality in whatever shape autonomous reason, volition, and emotion determine. Sin, instead of being viewed as an offense against a holy God, is seen merely as wrongs committed against other people, or simply as offenses against oneself. This requires a program for individual and social transformation, not the announcement of a divine rescue. Theologically, this combination of Pelagianism and anti-supernaturalism has swallowed much of Protestantism whole.

But today's evangelicals cannot simply point fingers at mainline denominations as harbors of this accommodation to modernity. In what remains, I would like to briefly indicate some of the ways in which this capitulation—usually unwitting and defended on the basis of reaching this generation of Christianity's "cultured despisers"—is realized in our own Babylonian captivity.

MODERNITY AND THE RISE OF THE NEW PELAGIANISM

Representing the first major counteroffensive against a thoroughly accommodated church, the Confessing Movement arose in Nazi Germany. Formed out of the Young Reformation League, this underground movement of young Lutheran and Reformed pastors eventually produced the Barmen Declaration. Whatever serious criticisms might be made of his project, Karl Barth was driven by a passion to dethrone the "sovereign self" of modernity, to drive back Pelagianism, and to glorify the God who rescues sinners by grace alone, through faith alone, because of Christ alone. Turning against his mentors, such as Adolf Harnack and Wilhelm Herrmann, both of whom claimed Luther as their spiritual father, Barth realized, as Athanasius and the Reformers had, that Christian proclamation had to be against the world in order to be for the world.

According to Herrmann, true communion with God is not found in the historical Jesus, insofar as his active and passive obedience fulfilled God's law on behalf of sinners and he was raised from the dead to the right hand of God. Rather, he said, it is to be found in the inner life of Jesus and its cultivation within oneself through pious devotion. On this side of the Atlantic, Princeton professor J. Gresham Machen, who had himself studied under Herrmann, similarly distinguished historic Christianity from modernism in his popular book, *Christianity and Liberalism*—which is still read in American history courses at Harvard. From their different perspectives, both writers reminded the church that what we are here calling the new Pelagianism is not merely a new version of Christianity, but a different religion altogether. But while many mainline Protestants are waking from their antidogmatic slumbers to rediscover the power of supernatural, redemptive Christianity, evangelicalism seems awash in a sea of human-centered religion.

Evangelicalism has gotten used to pitting itself against the older liberalism, even as it has also been quite self-conscious in distinguishing itself from a crude sort of fundamentalism. But what the movement has been less aware of, apparently, is the Pelagian current that runs deep and wide through its own terrain. While many nontheological factors are involved in this, and numerous individuals could be cited, there can be little doubt that the revivalist Charles Finney (1792–1875) represents a high-water mark of that stream. In his career, one already discerns a number of points at which a deeply religious Pelagianism and a secularized version of the same merge in the accommodation of contemporary evangelicalism to the culture of narcissism.

THE LEGACY OF CHARLES FINNEY

I recall wandering through the Billy Graham Center some years ago, observing the place of honor given to Finney in the evangelical tradition, reinforced by the first class in theology that I had at a Christian college, where Finney's work was required reading. Finney is particularly esteemed among the leaders of both the Christian Right and the Christian Left, by both Jerry Falwell and Jim Wallis, and his imprint can be seen in movements that appear to be diverse, but in reality are common heirs of Finney's legacy.

That is because the moralistic Finney envisioned a church that was in large measure an agency of personal and social reform, rather than an institution in which the means of grace, Word and sacrament, are made available to believers, who then take the gospel to the world. In the nineteenth century, while Southern evangelicalism was embroiled in slavery, Northern evangelicalism became increasingly identified with political causes—from abolition of slavery and child labor legislation to women's rights and the prohibition of alcohol. Despite their different political agendas, the South and the North shared a common commitment to revivalism. At the turn of the century, with an influx of Roman Catholic immigrants already making many American Protestants a bit uneasy, secularism began to pry the fingers of the Protestant establishment from the institutions (colleges, hospitals, and charitable organizations) they had created and sustained. In a desperate effort to regain this institutional power and the glory of "Christian America" (a vision that is always powerful in the imagination, but, after the disintegration of Puritan New England, remains elusive), the turn-of-the-century Protestant establishment launched campaigns to "Americanize" immigrants, to enforce moral instruction and "character education." Evangelists pitched their American gospel increasingly in terms of its practical usefulness to the individual and the nation.

That is at least one reason why Finney is so popular. He was the tallest marker in the shift from Reformation orthodoxy, evident in the Great Awakening (under Edwards and Whitefield), to Arminian (indeed, even Pelagian) revivalism, evident from the Second Great Awakening to the present. To demonstrate the debt of modern evangelicalism to Finney, we must first notice his theological departures. From these departures, Finney became the father of the antecedents to some of today's greatest challenges within the evangelical churches themselves, namely, the Church Growth Movement and political revivalism.

A Presbyterian lawyer, Finney one day experienced what he called "a mighty baptism of the Holy Ghost," which, *"like a wave of electricity,* going through and through me . . . seemed to come in *waves,* and *waves of liquid love."* The next morning, he informed his first client of the day, "I have a retainer from the Lord Jesus Christ to plead his cause, and I cannot plead yours."[2] Finney began conducting revivals in upstate New York. One of his most popular sermons was "Sinners Bound to Change Their Own Hearts."

Finney's one question for any given teaching was, "Is it fit to convert sinners with?" His "new measures" included the "anxious bench" (a precursor to today's altar call), emotional tactics that led to fainting, weeping, and other "excitements," as Finney and his followers called them. He became increasingly hostile toward Presbyterianism, referring (in the preface to his *Systematic Theology*[3]) to the Westminster Confession and its drafters as those who had created a paper pope, having "elevated their confession and catechism to the Papal throne and into the place of the Holy Ghost" (p. xii).

Remarkably, Finney demonstrates how close Arminian revivalism, in its naturalistic sentiments, tends to be to a more refined theological liberalism. Both cave in to the Enlightenment and its enthronement of the autonomous reason, will, and morality of the individual. Echoing the programmatic pronouncements of Lessing, Kant, and Hume, Finney declared, "That the instrument framed by that assembly should in the nineteenth century be recognized as the standard of the church, or of an intelligent branch of it, is not only amazing, but I must say that it is highly ridiculous. It is as absurd in theology as it would be in any other branch of science." "It is," said Finney, "better to have a living than a dead Pope" (p. xii).

One need go no further than the table of contents of his *Systematic Theology* to learn that Finney's theology revolved around human morality. Lectures 1 through 5 are on moral government, moral obligation, and the unity of moral action; lectures 6 and 7 are on obedience; and lectures 8 through 14 discuss love, selfishness, and virtues and vice in general. Not until lecture 21 does one read about anything that is especially Christian—the Atonement. This is followed by a discussion of regeneration, repentance, and faith. There is one lecture on justification, followed by six on sanctification. In other words, as Charles Hodge observed, Finney did not really write a systematic theology, but a collection of essays on ethics.

But that is not to say that Finney's *Systematic Theology* does not contain some significant theological statements. First, in answer to the question "Does a Christian cease to be a Christian, whenever he commits a sin?" Finney answers:

> Whenever he sins, he must, for the time being, cease to be holy. This is self-evident. Whenever he sins, he must be condemned; he must incur the penalty of the law of God. . . . If it be said that the precept is still binding upon him, but that with respect to the Christian, the penalty is forever set aside, or abrogated, I reply, that to abrogate the penalty is to repeal the precept; for a precept without penalty is no law. It is only counsel or advice. The Christian, therefore, is justified no longer than he obeys, and must be condemned when he disobeys; or Antinomianism is true. . . . In these respects, then, the sinning Christian and the unconverted sinner are upon precisely the same ground. (p. 46)

Finney believed that God demanded absolute perfection, but instead of that leading him to seek his perfect righteousness in Christ, he concluded that "full present obedience is a condition of justification." He continued:

> But again, to the question, can man be justified while sin remains in him? Surely he cannot, either upon legal or gospel principles, unless the law be repealed. . . . But can he be pardoned and accepted, and justified, in the gospel sense, while sin, any degree of sin, remains in him? Certainly not. (p. 57)

With the Westminster Confession in his sights, Finney declared of the Reformation's formula "simultaneously justified and sinful," "This error has slain more souls, I fear, than all the universalism that ever cursed the world." For "whenever a Christian sins he comes under condemnation, and must repent and do his first works, or be lost" (p. 60).

Finney's doctrine of justification rests upon a denial of the doctrine of original sin. Held by both Roman Catholics and Protestants, this biblical teaching insists that we are all born into this world inheriting Adam's guilt and corruption. We are, therefore, in bondage to a sinful nature. As someone has said, "We sin because we're sinners": the *condition* of sin is the source of specific *acts* of sin, rather than vice versa. But Finney followed Pelagius on this important point. Although he may never have been familiar with the Enlightenment, he was every bit as committed as any philosopher of the Enlightenment to many of the same arguments against the historic Christian understanding of human sinfulness. Finney believed that human beings are capable of choosing whether they will be corrupt or redeemed. He referred to original sin as an "anti-scriptural and nonsensical dogma" (p. 179). In clear terms, Finney denied the notion that human beings possess a sinful nature (p. 179). Therefore, if Adam leads us into sin, not by our inheriting his guilt and corruption, but by our following his poor example, then this leads logically to the view that Christ, the Second Adam, saves us by example. This is precisely where Finney takes it, in his explanation of the Atonement.

The first thing we must note about the Atonement, Finney says, is that Christ could not have died for anyone else's sins than his own. His obedience to the law and his perfect righteousness were sufficient to save him, but could not legally be accepted on behalf of others. That Finney's whole theology is driven by a passion for moral improvement is seen on this very point: "If he [Christ] had obeyed the law as our substitute, then why should our own return to personal obedience be insisted upon as a sine qua non of our salvation?" (p. 206). In other words, why would God insist that we save ourselves by our own obedience if Christ's work was sufficient? The reader should recall the words of Paul in this regard: "I do not nullify the grace of God; for if justification were through the law, then Christ died to no purpose" (Gal. 2:21). It would seem that Finney's reply would be one of agreement. The difference is that he had no difficulty believing that one can (and indeed must) be justified by obedience to the law.

That is not entirely fair, of course, because Finney did believe that Christ died for something—not for *someone,* but for *something.* In other words, he died for a purpose, but not for people. That purpose was to reassert God's moral government and lead us to eternal life by example, as Adam's example excited us to sin. Why did Christ die? God knew that

> the atonement would present to creatures the highest possible motives to virtue. Example is the highest moral influence that can be exerted. . . . If the benevolence manifested in the atonement does not subdue the selfishness of sinners, their case is hopeless. (p. 209)

Therefore, people are not helpless sinners who need to be redeemed, but wayward sinners who need a demonstration of selflessness so moving that they will be excited to stop being selfish. Finney did not just believe that the moral influence theory of the Atonement was the chief way of understanding the cross; he also explicitly denied the substitutionary theory of the Atonement, which

121

assumes that the atonement was a literal payment of a debt, which we have seen does not consist with the nature of the atonement. . . . It is true, that the atonement, of itself, does not secure the salvation of any one. (p. 217)

Then there is the matter of applying redemption. Throwing off the Calvinistic orthodoxy of the older Presbyterians and Congregationalists, Finney argued strenuously against the belief that the new birth is a divine gift, insisting that "regeneration consists in the sinner changing his ultimate choice, intention, preference; or in changing from selfishness to love or benevolence," as moved by the moral influence of Christ's example (p. 224). "Original or constitutional sinfulness, physical regeneration, and all their kindred and resulting dogmas, are alike subversive of the gospel, and repulsive to the human intelligence" (p. 236). Having nothing to do with original sin, substitutionary atonement, or a supernatural new birth, Finney proceeded to attack the doctrine of justification by grace alone through faith alone.

The Protestant Reformers insisted, on the basis of clear biblical texts, that justification was a forensic (i.e., legal) verdict. (In the Greek, literally, *to justify* means "to declare righteous," rather than "to make righteous"—a point that even Roman Catholic biblical scholars now recognize.) In other words, whereas Rome maintained that justification was a process of making a bad person better, the Reformers argued that it was a declaration or pronouncement that had someone else's righteousness (i.e., Christ's) as its basis. Therefore, it was a perfect, once-for-all verdict of right standing at the beginning of the Christian life, not in the middle or at the end.

The key words in the evangelical doctrine are *forensic* (meaning "legal") and *imputation* (meaning "crediting to one's account," as opposed to the idea of infusing a person's soul with righteousness). Thus, according to the evangelical expression, sinners are justified *sola fide propter solum Christum*—"by faith alone on the basis of Christ alone." Christ's righteousness is the only ground and God-given faith is the only instrument of justification. Knowing all of this, Finney declares:

> But *for sinners to be forensically pronounced just, is impossible and absurd.* . . . As we shall see, there are *many conditions,* while there is but one ground, of the justification of sinners. . . . As has already been said, there can be no justification in a legal or forensic sense, but *upon the ground of universal, perfect, and uninterrupted obedience to law.* This is of course denied by those who hold that gospel justification, or the justification of penitent sinners, is of the nature of a forensic or judicial justification. They hold to the legal maxim that what a man does by another he does by himself, and therefore the law regards Christ's obedience as ours, on the ground that he obeyed for us. (emphasis added)

To this, Finney replies: "The doctrine of an imputed righteousness, or that Christ's obedience to the law was accounted as our obedience, is founded on a most false and nonsensical assumption"—namely, the substitutionary Atonement. After all, Christ's righteousness "could do no more than justify himself. It can never be imputed to us. . . . It was naturally impossible, then, for him to obey in our behalf." This "representing of the atonement as the ground of the sinner's justification has been a sad occasion of stumbling to many" (pp. 320–22). The view that faith is the sole condition of justification is "the antinomian view," Finney asserts. "We shall see that perseverance in obedience to the end of life is also a condition of justification." Furthermore,

> Present sanctification, in the sense of present full consecration to God, is another condition . . . of justification. Some theologians have made justification a condition of sanctification, instead of making sanctification a condition of justification. But this we shall see is an erroneous view of the subject. (pp. 326–27)

Each act of sin requires "a fresh justification" (p. 331). Referring to "the framers of the Westminster Confession of faith," and their view of an imputed righteousness, Finney wonders, "If this is not antinomianism, I know not what is" (p. 332). The "theory" of what Luther called "this marvelous exchange" is unreasonable to Finney, so he concludes, "I regard these dogmas as fabulous, and better befitting a romance than a system of theology" (p. 333). He concludes this section against the Westminster Assembly by shrewdly observing the necessary connection between the evangelical understanding of sin and the correlative need for a radical redemption:

> The relations of the old school view of justification to their view of depravity is obvious. They hold, as we have seen, that the constitution in every faculty and part is sinful. Of course, a return to personal, present holiness, in the sense of entire conformity to the law, cannot with them be a condition of justification. They must have a justification while yet at least in some degree of sin. This must be brought about by imputed righteousness. The intellect revolts at a justification in sin. So a scheme is devised to divert the eye

of the law and of the lawgiver from the sinner to his substitute, who has perfectly obeyed the law. (p. 339)

This he calls "another gospel."

As the Princeton theologian B. B. Warfield pointed out so eloquently, there are two religions throughout history: naturalism ("heathenism"), of which Pelagianism is a religious expression, and supernatural redemption.[4] And with Warfield and others who so seriously warned their brothers and sisters of these errors held by Finney and his successors,[5] we too must come to terms with this wildly heterodox strain in American Protestantism. Sharing roots in Finney's revivalism, perhaps evangelical and liberal Protestantism are not that far apart after all. His "new measures," like today's Church Growth Movement, made human choices and emotions the center of the church's ministry, ridiculed theology, and replaced the preaching of Christ with the preaching of conversion.

It is in Finney's naturalistic moralism that Christian political and social crusades find their faith in humanity and its resources in self-salvation. Sounding not a little like a deist, Finney declared:

There is nothing in religion beyond the ordinary powers of nature. It consists entirely in the right exercise of the powers of nature. It is just that, and nothing else. When mankind become truly religious, they are not enabled to put forth exertions which they were unable before to put forth. They only exert powers which they had before, in a different way, and use them for the glory of God.[6]

Thus, as the new birth is a natural phenomenon, so too is a revival: "A revival is not a miracle, nor dependent on a miracle, in any sense. It is a purely philosophical result of the right use of the constituted means—as much so as any other effect produced by the application of means." The belief that the new birth and revival depend necessarily on divine activity is pernicious. "No doctrine," he says, "is more dangerous than this to the prosperity of the Church, and nothing more absurd."[7] When the leaders of the Church Growth Movement claim that theology gets in the way of growth, and when they insist that it does not matter what a particular church believes, since growth is a matter of following the proper principles, they are displaying their debt to Finney. When leaders of various movements praise as "revival" the barking, roaring, screaming, laughing, and other strange phenomena on the basis that "it works," insisting that one must judge its truth by its fruit, they are following Finney—as well as the father of American pragmatism, William James, who declared that truth must be judged on the basis of "its cash-value in experiential terms." And when evangelicals follow Finney's tradition in subverting theological clarity in the service of moral and political causes, they are treading the same well-worn path of Finney's late nineteenth-century heirs who shaped mainline Protestantism into the movement that H. Richard Niebuhr captured with such tragic poignancy: "A God without wrath brought men without sin into a kingdom without judgment through the ministrations of a Christ without a cross."[8]

Thus, in Finney's theology, God is not sovereign, man is not a sinner by nature, the Atonement is not a true payment for sin, justification by imputation is insulting to reason and morality, the new birth is simply the effect of successful techniques, and revival is a natural result of clever campaigns. In his foreword to the bicentennial edition of Finney's *Systematic Theology,* Harry Conn commends Finney's pragmatism:

"Many servants of our Lord should be diligently searching for a gospel that 'works,' and I am happy to state they can find it in this volume."[9]

Finney did not only abandon the material principle of the Reformation (justification), making him a renegade from evangelical Christianity. He also repudiated doctrines, such as original sin and the substitutionary Atonement, that have been embraced by Roman Catholics and Protestants alike. Therefore, Finney was not merely an Arminian, but a Pelagian. He was not only an enemy of evangelical Protestantism, but of historic Christianity in its broadest sense. I have no doubt that the Protestant Reformers would have found themselves more at home at the Council of Trent than in the precincts of America's Counter-Reformation.

It is important to add, after all of this, that modern evangelicalism is hardly monolithic, either in its Reformation theology or in its Pelagianism. In fact, the movement is a broad confluence of these two radically opposed traditions. Hopefully, even Arminian readers of Finney's statements cited above recoil in disapproval, as indeed Arminius and Wesley no doubt would have done. But this is where the rub comes: are we willing to recognize the extent to which the *theology* of America's Counter-Reformation determines the *practice* of evangelism, church growth, and understandings of revival and the Christian life? It is at this point that the most confusion lies. There are Reformed and Presbyterian churches that would wholeheartedly endorse the evangelical doctrine of their confession and catechisms, while denying—or at least weakening—their power in shaping their ministry, worship, and outreach. Many of our churches are theoretically Reformed, yet more humanistic in their practical orientation.

Wherever the reader finds himself on the ecclesiastical

map, it should be relatively easy to recognize that a Pelagianizing tendency has worked its way into the fabric of American religion. If secularism (as distinct from secularization) is a religion of naturalism, then isn't it at least conceivable that the secularization of the mainline and increasingly the evangelical churches is in some sense the result of the triumph of Finney-style religion that is then secularized and fed back to the churches as pragmatism, therapy, sentimentalism, narcissism, consumerism, and other marks of modernity? To be sure, there are other causes, but isn't it the case that we have to some degree been digging our own grave in American evangelicalism? If, as I suggest, at least part of the challenge to a serious witness to human sinfulness and radical divine grace is a distorted theology that, after profoundly shaping the culture, has then been secularized and marketed back to the churches as a requirement for contemporary mission, what is that culture which a secularized Pelagianism produces?

THE CULTURE OF NARCISSISM: NAMING THE WHIRLWIND

We cannot reject everything in the modern world, including secular culture, without denying God's common grace. At the same time, we cannot embrace modernity uncritically, because it is mired in human rebellion (including our own), belonging to "this fading evil age." While avoiding an easy antimodernism, we need to recognize that our lives and cultural habits are largely shaped by an obsession with the self to an unprecedented degree in our day. While self-obsession has an ancient pedigree in the human heart, it has perhaps never been so widely justified and praised as a virtue, at least by professing Christians.

A typical expression among sociologists and historians for this pervasive tendency is "the sovereign self." It was Nietzsche who first spoke so eloquently (and supportively) of the "weightlessness" of God in Western culture, and I am not the first to regard this phenomenon as being cashed out in the following dominant expressions:

1. *The therapeutic self.* This term, coined by Philip Reiff, captures well what Christopher Lasch meant in *The Culture of Narcissism* when he spoke of "transcendental self-attention." What this means for religion, said Lasch, is that "the new narcissist is haunted not by guilt but by anxiety."[10] A host of consequences emerge, such as the disdain for sustained thought in favor of immediate experience:

> Our culture's indifference to the past—which easily shades over into active hostility and rejection—furnishes the most telling proof of that culture's bankruptcy. . . . A denial of the past, superficially progressive and optimistic, proves on closer analysis to embody the despair of a society that cannot face the future.[11]

Can we not say the same of America's churches, generally speaking? In this context, the self is viewed as essentially innocent, a divine spark that has been thrown mercilessly into an alien creation, the victim of nature, nurture, and history. Reacting sharply against traditional Christian insistence on the sinfulness of creatures made in God's image and their dependence on God, therapeutic dogmatics rests upon a foundation of human goodness and autonomy. If the self is needy rather than sinful, the remedy is obviously recovery rather than redemption. Guilt is out; vulnerability is in. Similarly, hearing God's announcement of judgment and justification is often replaced with "sharing" with each other in small groups. "The contemporary climate," Lasch hardly has to remind us, "is therapeutic, not religious. People today hunger not for personal salvation, let alone for the restoration of an earlier golden age, but for the feeling, the momentary illusion, of personal well-being, health, and psychic security."[12] And churches across the theological spectrum also cater increasingly to those who, for all practical purposes, are convinced that there is only one life to live.

2. *The pragmatic self.* William James was at least descriptively accurate when he urged, "God is not believed, he is used." Again, this is not unique to modernity, since "God" has been exploited even by the church for cultural, racial, economic, and religious causes since Adam and Eve "saw that the tree was desirable to the eyes and useful to make one wise." But Americans have been masters of technique: getting things done is our specialty—even if we don't always understand the problem or the goal. As in the therapeutic orientation, the pragmatic self aims at mastery, assuming the position of the sun in the constellation of cause and effect. If one can just come up with the right technique, the problem— whatever it is—can be solved. Thus, all values, all goals, all goods, and all convictions are judged, as James said concerning religious claims, "by their cash-value in experiential terms." Awed by the incredible technological sophistication that we see all around us, we envision our faith in parallel terms, as a sort of spiritual technology. As in the therapeutic paradigm, it is easy to push God out of the picture, as Finney did by calling revival and the new birth nothing more than "the right use of means."

3. *The self as consumer.* Economies of exchange have existed since the dawn of human culture, but this may be the first era in which people view themselves as consumers. As with the therapeutic and pragmatic layers of modern consciousness, there are many factors involved, and perhaps only a few of them are theological. But the theological factors have been essential in contributing to a spiritual environment in which the sense of oneself as a moral self, with certain duties to family, church, neighborhood, and society, has largely given way to the commodification of reality: everything has a price. (It is worth noting American evangelist Billy Sunday's boast that he could guarantee results at two dollars per soul.) "The business of America is business," said Andrew Carnegie. In this environment, it is difficult for us to resist the temptation to regard "reality" as entirely constructed, largely by us, from a collage of clippings taken from myriad advertisements. Instead of thinking of ourselves and others chiefly as believers and unbelievers, we increasingly see things in terms of sellers and buyers. Religious experience is a valuable commodity in today's global economy, but trading on the "Big Board" has its own price tag, as God is increasingly made in our image. Felt needs easily mask real needs in a culture of consumerism, so that regardless of what one believes on paper, the category of sinners saved by grace is replaced by that of customers reached by marketing. If the self—particularly, the self as chooser—is sovereign, then a secularized Pelagianism controls our ministry.

EVANGELICALS AND "THE CRISIS"

Now the question is not whether we try to roll back the clock to some golden age that never was, but whether we take serious stock of the remarkable secularity of our culture that so many of us seem to regard as neutral. Like our unbelieving neighbors, we seem these days to regard these cultural habits only as opportunities. It is not our evangelistic passion that needs to be challenged, but our often uncritical appropriation of modernity as a passive conduit for reaching the world for Christ.

The real question is whether we still believe that the gospel is "the power of God for salvation." There are Calvinists and Lutherans out there who subscribe to the belief that salvation, from beginning to end, is God's work, and yet they seem to profess otherwise in their willingness to hide the offense of the Cross, to transform the prickly biblical categories and replace their content with something more culturally "relevant" (read: "acceptable"). But the only theological perspective that we find naturally attractive is the one in which our own guilt is minimized, our goodness is affirmed, encouragement for self-improvement is offered, and the promise of "salvation" (in this life or the next) is credited to our success. Many of us who would inveigh against "works righteousness" in Roman Catholicism, for instance, utterly miss it under our own Protestant nose. The theology that we profess when signing our names to a creed and confession is mere assent if it does not actually shape our faith and practice.

In North America, the term *evangelical* once included the followers of both Charles Wesley, an Arminian, and George Whitefield, a Calvinist. But in America's Second Great Awakening, especially in the wake of Finney, a well-documented shift, not only to an extreme form of Arminianism, but from theology in general to the individual's experience and personal choice, transformed the very character of evangelicalism.

Even in its doctrinal minimalism, the evangelical movement in America after World War II seemed to affirm, often
at great risk, the authority, clarity, and sufficiency of Scripture, original sin, the substitutionary Atonement, justification,
the need for supernatural conversion, and the reality of a final
judgment that, with all of its acknowledged emotional difficulty, included hell. Furthermore, the laity seemed to be as
convinced as their leaders of these positions and could explain
them to others. But in the name of "mission" (i.e., having influence in American culture), the evangelical movement in
America today risks driving out any serious concern for truth.
Evangelicals want to be mainstream and well-liked—the
movement's Achilles' heel. And when it gets us on the cover
of *The Atlantic Monthly,* we feel vindicated.

RESTORING AN EVANGELICAL CONSENSUS: IS IT POSSIBLE?

The divide in contemporary evangelicalism is not between
Arminianism and Calvinism. My Lutheran colleagues with
whom I have collaborated for some time now do not accept all
of my Calvinistic tenets, either. But does God, as Friedrich
Nietzsche and David Wells have argued, rest lightly upon our
shoulders today? And if so, is it possible that this has been
abetted by a humanistic theological orientation among us that
reaches beyond Arminianism to Pelagianism—even among
some who hold in theory to an Augustinian theology?

For many of us, framing the issue in this way can only
mean that ours is a debate between moralism and Christianity. One is a religion of good advice, and the other is a religion
of good news. One celebrates the culture of narcissism, and

the other knocks the wind out of us by making us face the truth about ourselves for once and then gives us new wind as we are personally addressed with the announcement that we never thought was possible. Some of us believe that whenever religion declines, there is a rising esteem for the human capacity for self-salvation. God goes down in human estimation, and humanity rises. It's the way of the world. And when it becomes the way of the church, the salt has lost its savor.

Many have seen the work of the Alliance of Confessing Evangelicals as merely throwing out worn slogans from a bygone era: Scripture alone, Christ alone, grace alone, faith alone, to the glory of God alone. But for others, they represent the great affirmations of historic Christianity, which alone can ensure that the good news is good indeed. Scripture is clear, which makes our divisions all the more deplorable. Its clarity focuses on the history of God's redeeming grace in Jesus Christ, issued in that authoritative and binding address of law and gospel. This ends the presumed mastery of the "sovereign self." In fact, it is not even the case that the self is responsible for its own dethronement, surrendering mastery to God. Rather, God himself does this by announcing our judgment in the law, burying us with Christ by baptism into death, and raising us up with Christ in newness of life.

Baptism into Christ is the radical paradigm that displaces the mastery of the sovereign self, reorienting our misshapen existence and ministry to a world in such great need. Through the law, we became conscious of our sin, and through the gospel we were justified and are being sanctified. It is because God has done all of this, from beginning to end, that he alone can be glorified; it is all of grace. And it turns us inside out, away from the obsession with self and the inner life, outward to Christ, and, through Christ, to our vocation in the world.

An "outward-bound" theology should lead to an "outward-bound" ethic. By being properly named ("sinner," "outsider," "enemy of God") and graciously renamed in Christ ("saint," "coheir," "son"), a new creation and a new community are born. Sin is now foremost an offense against God, then an offense against one's neighbor, and only then an offense against oneself. Consequently, reconciliation follows that new order as well. The tyranny of modern selfhood is finally transcended. The Other speaks; the self listens.

So is it likely that an evangelical consensus can be restored? Only God knows the answer to that question. We may be witnessing a new sort of ecumenism, in which churches matter more than movements and our distinct confessions are allowed to enrich wider discussion rather than being seen as a hindrance to hazy minimalism.

One thing is for sure: unity has never been a good rallying point for unity. No great movements seem to have ever coalesced voluntarily around unity. But the force for Christian unity is the gospel and, wrapped around it, the whole teaching of Scripture. Unity is a gift of the Spirit, as people agree in the truth. But to agree in the truth, we have to talk about the truth and perhaps even argue about it. May God give us the grace, the charity, the patience, and the courage to love each other enough to pursue that truth, wherever it leads, and to joyfully accept the unity that it generates—however humble it may be in the eyes of the world.

7

IRRESISTIBLE GRACE

DOUGLAS J. WILSON

The language of irresistible grace is both odd and obvious. It is odd because we never speak this way in comparable situations. It is obvious as soon as it is stated carefully, making the expression redundant. This is reminiscent of one of C. S. Lewis's Dufflepuds, who said that water was powerful wet stuff. And thus we learn to see grace as irresistible stuff.

When God shows his kindness to us, he is showing that kindness to *creatures*. We are beings who at one time had no being. The world, of which we are a part, at one time had no being. When God acted in creation, he did so *ex nihilo*. The heavens and earth, the stars and pebbles, the trees and galaxies, and the toads and lions were all fashioned as a result of the divine word. Nothing was made apart from Jesus

Christ (John 1:3), and it is by faith that we understand that the worlds were framed out of that which cannot be seen (Heb. 11:3).

And so we speak of creation. But no one speaks of the doctrine of irresistible creation. However, when we think about it for a moment, we should realize that *creatio ex nihilo* is about as irresistible as it gets. Was there any likelihood that nonexistent matter was going to defy God when he summoned the universe into being?

It is the same with the grace of the new creation:

> But if our gospel be hid, it is hid to them that are lost: in whom the god of this world hath blinded the minds of them which believe not, lest the light of the glorious gospel of Christ, who is the image of God, should shine unto them. For we preach not ourselves, but Christ Jesus the Lord; and ourselves your servants for Jesus' sake. For God, who commanded the light to shine out of darkness, hath shined in our hearts, to give the light of the knowledge of the glory of God in the face of Jesus Christ. (2 Cor. 4:3–6)

The God who summoned light from darkness at the beginning, without consulting the wishes of darkness, is the same God who summoned the light in our souls into being. He is the Creator, and he is the New Creator. And when he creates, he does so according to form. Creation, by definition, is irresistible. This is so obvious that we never speak of it this way.

Birth is another irresistible process. As writers in another time would have said, the present writer was born in 1953. I do not recall being consulted about this in 1952, and I have it on good authority that this was because I was not there. I was born a Wilson, and not a Smith. I was born a boy, and not a girl. I was born in the United States, and not in Ethiopia. I had all kinds of irresistible things thrust at me, and did not begin to seriously reflect on what I was doing with it all until about sixteen years later.

Scripture describes our entry into the kingdom of God as a new birth:

> Jesus answered and said unto him, Verily, verily, I say unto thee, Except a man be born again, he cannot see the kingdom of God. Nicodemus saith unto him, How can a man be born when he is old? can he enter the second time into his mother's womb, and be born? Jesus answered, Verily, verily, I say unto thee, Except a man be born of water and of the Spirit, he cannot enter into the kingdom of God. That which is born of the flesh is flesh; and that which is born of the Spirit is spirit. Marvel not that I said unto thee, Ye must be born again. The wind bloweth where it listeth, and thou hearest the sound thereof, but canst not tell whence it cometh, and whither it goeth: so is every one that is born of the Spirit. (John 3:3–8)

This profoundly rich passage includes an allusion to the rebirth of Israel as the new Israel, the church—which Ezekiel prophesied, and which Nicodemus should have known about. The passage also includes the basic spiritual truth that "the wind bloweth where it listeth." We cannot manipulate the reality of new life—and yet we like to pretend we can. Modern evangelicals talk much about the new birth, and they instruct people on how to be born again, and they take them through it step-by-step. In many ways, the doctrine of regeneration is a signature issue for modern evangelicals, and the third chapter of John is frequently quoted. But the summary statement that Jesus makes here is routinely ignored. We cannot tell where the wind is coming from or where it is going. The Greek words for "wind" and "Spirit" in this passage are the same word, and so the illustration from the wind is a particularly apt one. But we have come to believe that we can capture that breeze and lock it in an aerosol can to be dispensed on demand during evangelistic encounters. But Jesus taught that this was exactly what the new birth was not like.

No one writes books on how to be born the first time. Who would buy one? Where is the market for such a thing? And this is why, in order to explain to people the steps they must go through in order to be born *again,* we have to ignore one of the central aspects of this metaphor of birth. Birth is mysterious and irresistible. Because we understand this about birth, we rarely have to make the point. "Where were you born?" is a common question. No one replies, "San Diego. Irresistibly." We never say this because it is so obvious.

But we do need to think about it some more, and apply it to our understanding of our spiritual life—which is from the hand of God as inexorably as is our physical life. In fact, the Scriptures expressly compare the two kinds of life at just this point. But because of spiritual pride, we still want to take some credit for our spiritual life. If this new life is purely a gift, then there is no room for boasting. Over against this self-willed attitude, the Bible speaks plainly: "Of his own will begat he us with the word of truth, that we should be a kind of firstfruits of his creatures" (James 1:18). Notice that the seed of our life is the word of truth, that the fact of our life proceeds from the will of the God who begat us, and that he did so in order that we would be the firstfruits among his creatures.

Resurrection is another irresistible reality in God's world:

Jesus saith unto her, Said I not unto thee, that, if thou wouldest believe, thou shouldest see the glory of God? Then they took away the stone from the place where the dead was laid. And Jesus lifted up his eyes, and said, Father, I thank thee that thou hast heard me. And I knew that thou hearest me always: but because of the people which stand by I said it, that they may believe that thou hast sent me. And when he thus had spoken, he cried with a loud voice, Lazarus, come forth. And he that was dead came forth, bound hand and foot with graveclothes: and his face was bound about with a napkin. Jesus saith unto them, Loose him, and let him go. (John 11:40–44)

Now when Jesus performed this miracle, he did not first have to secure the cooperation of Lazarus. Rather, the miracle *resulted* in the cooperation of Lazarus. After he was raised from the dead, Lazarus did all the hopping and all the mumbling through the grave clothes. But prior to the resurrecting word of authority, Lazarus was simply dead, to state it simply. The raising of Lazarus was not a cooperative effort between Christ and Lazarus.

It should not be surprising that the arrival of grace in our lives is described by Scripture as a resurrection:

Therefore we are buried with him by baptism into death: that like as Christ was raised up from the dead by the glory of the Father, even so we also should walk in newness of life. . . . Now if we be dead with Christ, we believe that we shall also live with him. (Rom. 6:4, 8)

But we have seen that resurrections, in the very nature of the case, require a previously dead person. This dead person, obviously, does not have a lot to contribute toward bringing himself back to life. He's dead; only God can give him new life:

> And you hath he quickened, who were dead in trespasses and sins; wherein in time past ye walked according to the course of this world, according to the prince of the power of the air, the spirit that now worketh in the children of disobedience: among whom also we all had our conversation in times past in the lusts of our flesh, fulfilling the desires of the flesh and of the mind; and were by nature the children of wrath, even as others. But God, who is rich in mercy, for his great love wherewith he loved us, even when we were dead in sins, hath quickened us together with Christ, (by grace ye are saved;) and hath raised us up together, and made us sit together in heavenly places in Christ Jesus: that in the ages to come he might shew the exceeding riches of his grace in his kindness toward us through Christ Jesus. For by grace are ye saved through faith; and that not of yourselves: it is the gift of God: not of works, lest any man should boast. For we are his workmanship, created in Christ Jesus unto good works, which God hath before ordained that we should walk in them. (Eph. 2:1–10)

In this passage, the progression of Paul's argument leads directly to his conclusions concerning the nature of grace and how it excludes boasting. No doubt Lazarus told Mary and Martha afterwards about what it felt like to be raised, but we really cannot reconstruct that conversation. However, we can be sure that Lazarus did not say that while Jesus pulled and pulled, he, Lazarus, pushed and pushed, until there he was, alive again.

Pagan unbelievers were physically alive—they walked according to the course of this world, which implies movement. But they were walking in a condition of spiritual death. Paul says twice that God raised those who were dead in their sins, quickening them with Christ. This (and only this) is the basis for saying that "by grace ye are saved." We are saved by grace—it is the gift of God. Because it is a display of resurrection power, there is no possibility of boasting. We are not saved by anything we have said, thought, or done in our condition of death. If we were, then far from being an argument that we contribute to our resurrection, it would instead be an argument that we are already alive and do not need a resurrection.

While we are not saved by our good works, we are saved to do good works. This is because we are *God's* workmanship, *created* in Christ Jesus. There it is again, God being God, and creation being what it always has to be, which is, utterly dependent upon God.

Once these truths are grasped, it makes the common language of Scripture much easier to accept at face value. The Bible speaks of these realities constantly. Sometimes it does so with resurrecting grace at the center of the discussion, and sometimes it does so in passing. When we see the glory of grace, we start to see this glory everywhere. "Who also hath made us able ministers of the new testament; not of the letter, but of the spirit: for the letter killeth, but the spirit giveth life" (2 Cor. 3:6). There it is. The Spirit gives life, and when he has not given life, it is not present and cannot be present.

The Holy Spirit is the agent of God's grace. He is the one who brings that grace to bear at the moment a man is converted to God. God the Father is the one who elected us before the foundation of the world, and God the Son is the one who shed his blood to secure our forgiveness, and the Holy Spirit is the one who calls us into the obedience of faith and sanctifies us. Peter refers to every aspect of our Trinitarian salvation: "Elect according to the foreknowledge of God the Father, through sanctification of the Spirit, unto obedience and sprinkling of the blood of Jesus Christ: Grace unto you, and peace, be multiplied" (1 Peter 1:2).

We are put right with God on the basis of his mercy toward us. "Not by works of righteousness which we have done, but according to his mercy he saved us, by the washing of regeneration, and renewing of the Holy Ghost" (Titus 3:5).

When God gives us the grace of a new heart, the first thing we do with it is to repent and believe. And this is why the Scriptures speak of repentance and belief as gifts—they are actions which we perform, but which require the prior gift of life. We are accustomed to hearing it said that people are to repent and believe, so that they might be born again. They are to repent and believe with their old heart, so that God will give them a new heart. But if the old heart is capable of repentance and faith, which is all that God requires of us, then why do we need a new heart?

God is the one who opens hearts, and this leads to repentance and faith. "And when the Gentiles heard this, they were glad, and glorified the word of the Lord: and as many as were ordained to eternal life believed" (Acts 13:48). Again: "And a certain woman named Lydia, a seller of purple, of the city of Thyatira, which worshipped God, heard us: whose heart the Lord opened, that she attended unto the things which were spoken of Paul" (Acts 16:14). God opened this woman's heart, and that is why she listened. That is why she repented. That is why she believed.

And that is also why the Bible speaks so plainly about the

gift of repentance. Repentance is not the coin we put in the vending machine of salvation to get our product. Repentance is part of the gift. "Him hath God exalted with his right hand to be a Prince and a Saviour, for *to give repentance to Israel,* and forgiveness of sins" (Acts 5:31). But God did not limit this gracious gift to Israel alone; he offered it to Gentiles as well: "When they heard these things, they held their peace, and glorified God, saying, *Then hath God also to the Gentiles granted repentance unto life"* (Acts 11:18).

This is why we are to conduct ourselves with meekness toward those who oppose the gospel. This is one of the instruments that God uses to give that repentance. "In meekness instructing those that oppose themselves; *if God peradventure will give them repentance* to the acknowledging of the truth; and that they may recover themselves out of the snare of the devil, who are taken captive by him at his will" (2 Tim. 2:25–26).

Faith is a gift as well, and it rests upon the same foundation. "All that the Father giveth me shall come to me; and him that cometh to me I will in no wise cast out" (John 6:37). Scripture expressly declares that our faith in God is a gift from him. This is because faith is the natural fruit of the new heart, in its turn a gift from God. "For unto you it is *given* in the behalf of Christ, *not only to believe* on him, but also to suffer for his sake" (Phil. 1:29). The Philippians had been given the gift of faith and the gift of suffering.

In the same way, Apollos was a tremendous encouragement to the saints, but the way in which those saints are described is interesting:

And when he was disposed to pass into Achaia, the brethren wrote, exhorting the disciples to receive him: who, when he was come, helped them much *which had believed through grace:* for he mightily convinced the Jews, and that publickly, shewing by the scriptures that Jesus was Christ. (Acts 18:27–28)

It does not say that they had believed in grace, or that they had been helped by grace. Rather, the text is plain—their belief was the result of God's grace to them.

This kindness from God begins in our lives at the point that theologians call the effectual call. The Bible uses the word *call* in different ways. One usage is that of naming: "He called his name JESUS" (Matt. 1:25). Another use has the sense of an invitation that can be declined, as in "Many are called, but few are chosen" (Matt. 22:14).

But in the overwhelming number of instances, Scripture describes God's calling of his people as an efficacious call—a call that secures and settles. This is why believers are identified as "the called." They are the ones on whom this irresistible gift has been bestowed.

"Among whom are ye also *the called* of Jesus Christ: to all that be in Rome, beloved of God, called to be saints: Grace to you and peace from God our Father, and the Lord Jesus Christ" (Rom. 1:6–7). That this goes far beyond mere invitation is plain. "Moreover whom he did predestinate, them he also *called:* and whom he called, them he also justified: and whom he justified, them he also glorified" (Rom. 8:30). Those who are predestined are called, those who are called are justified, and those who are justified are glorified. To think that such a passage could include a proviso that "those whom he called, he also lamented when they left" is to ignore the entire progression of Paul's thought.

"Unto the church of God which is at Corinth, to them that

are sanctified in Christ Jesus, *called to be saints,* with all that in every place call upon the name of Jesus Christ our Lord, both theirs and ours" (1 Cor. 1:2). When the Holy Spirit calls in this sense, he accomplishes what he calls for. "God is faithful, *by whom ye were called* unto the fellowship of his Son Jesus Christ our Lord" (1 Cor. 1:9).

This calling was settled before the world began, but is issued in the world of history. "Who hath saved us, *and called us with an holy calling,* not according to our works, but according to his own purpose and grace, which was given us in Christ Jesus before the world began" (2 Tim. 1:9). God's grace was given to us in his counsel before the world was fashioned, but we were summoned into fellowship with him—when the time was right—by his effectual, efficacious, irresistible, and holy call. "There is one body, and one Spirit, even as ye are called in one hope of your calling" (Eph. 4:4).

When God calls, the dead hear it. When God speaks, his word creates ears so that creatures can hear what he said. And this is why we are the called. "Jude, the servant of Jesus Christ, and brother of James, to them that are sanctified by God the Father, and preserved in Jesus Christ, *and called*" (Jude 1). We are called to holiness, and this holiness includes the understanding that we do not control the machinery of our salvation. "But as he which hath called you is holy, so be ye holy in all manner of conversation" (1 Peter 1:15). We are called to holiness, and this includes all aspects of our life. This includes the humble understanding that we are creatures, and that we would have no standing before God at all unless he had given it. When we receive this in all humility, we learn that the humble are lifted up—just as God promises throughout his Word. We are summoned to glory, called to it: "But the God of all grace, *who hath called us unto his eternal glory* by Christ

Jesus, after that ye have suffered a while, make you perfect, stablish, strengthen, settle you" (1 Peter 5:10). This call is not thwarted because it is a call to eternal life. When God calls forth a bride for his Son, when he sends his Spirit out to bring back a bride for his Son, he does not do so with the air of a shy and hapless suitor. His call is a summons. "According as his divine power hath given unto us all things that pertain unto life and godliness, through the knowledge of him that hath *called us to glory and virtue*" (2 Peter 1:3).

This is a call that not only brings us to salvation, but also throws down every human attempt to manufacture some sort of acceptable self-righteousness. We are commanded to glory in our salvation, just as Lazarus no doubt gloried in the power of the Lord when he spoke with his loved ones on the evening of his first day back. And when we glory in the Lord, there is no room for self-glory. We must glorify the Lord down to the ground—and beneath the ground, where all the dead bodies are.

> But we preach Christ crucified, unto the Jews a stumbling-block, and unto the Greeks foolishness; but unto them which are called, both Jews and Greeks, Christ the power of God, and the wisdom of God. Because the foolishness of God is wiser than men; and the weakness of God is stronger than men. For ye see your calling, brethren, how that not many wise men after the flesh, not many mighty, not many noble, are called: but God hath chosen the foolish things of the world to confound the wise; and God hath chosen the weak things of the world to confound the things which are mighty; and base things of the world, and things which are despised, hath God chosen, yea, and things which are not, to bring to nought things that are: that no flesh should glory in his presence. But of him are ye in

Christ Jesus, who of God is made unto us wisdom, and righteousness, and sanctification, and redemption: that, according as it is written, He that glorieth, let him glory in the Lord. (1 Cor. 1:23–31)

God chooses "things which are not" in order to bring to nothing "things that are." He does this so that no one might glory in his presence. These are the things revealed to babes, so that the one who glories may glory in the Lord. We do this simply—by understanding through the gift of humility that God is God and we are not. He gives us eyes, and it is afterward that we can see. He gives us a mouth to praise him, and afterward we sing psalms. He gives life, and then we may walk away from the tomb—and not a moment before. We do not see and then get eyes for a reward. We do not hear and then receive the gift of ears. We do not walk around a bit to show that we are good candidates for resurrection.

Life is grace, and grace is life. Works are death, and the dead perform their helpless works. The sovereign Lord took Ezekiel into the valley filled with bones.

"Can these bones live?"

"Ah, sovereign Lord, you know."

"Son of man," he said, "preach to the bones."

Ezekiel preached the way a man of God must preach. We are not here to give candies to the healthy or medicine to the sick. We are in the middle of a bleak and desolate graveyard, and we serve a God who raises the dead. He does so by means of his Word, which is the incorruptible seed, and which we are privileged to declare. And as we do, the dead are raised. Irresistibly.

8

SOLUS CHRISTUS

JOHN F. MACARTHUR

Is it possible that some non-Christians might go to heaven when they die, or are those without Christ totally cut off from God and without hope in the world (cf. Eph. 2:12)?

Scripture gives us an unequivocal answer to that question: "He who believes in the Son has everlasting life; and he who does not believe the Son shall not see life, but the wrath of God abides on him" (John 3:36). Salvation from eternal condemnation is by faith alone (*sola fide*), and Christ alone (*solus Christus*) saves. Apart from Christ, there is no hope for anyone. Jesus himself taught, "I am the way, the truth, and the life. No one comes to the Father except through Me" (John 14:6). The apostle Peter said, "Nor is there salvation in any other, for there is no other name under heaven given among men by which we must be saved" (Acts 4:12).

Evangelicals in previous generations consistently affirmed that truth, and they correctly regarded it as essential to authentic Christianity. The conviction that there is no possibility of heaven apart from faith in Christ has motivated our evangelistic efforts, it has spawned the great missionary movements, and it has been more or less what makes evangelicals *evangelical*. The truth of "Christ alone"—*solus Christus*—is the very heart of the gospel. Our spiritual ancestors grounded their faith in that. They based their teaching on it. And they filled their preaching with it. That is the evangelical heritage.

But lately, the term *evangelical* has all but lost its historic meaning. The boundaries of "evangelicalism" are systematically being enlarged to be as inclusive as possible. Consequently, the evangelical movement as a whole no longer speaks with clarity about the exclusivity of Christ. A few well-known evangelical leaders have even begun to suggest that Jews, Roman Catholics, Hindus, Moslems, and devout people from other religions might be admitted to heaven after all, if they are sincere enough or good enough in following what they believe. Of course, that is just what Socinians, deists, universalists, and liberals have always believed—and what historic evangelicalism has always stood against. But now, in the name of postmodern tolerance, the camel of universalism has got its nose under the evangelical tent.

One recent book, written by a well-known evangelical pastor and published by a mainstream evangelical press, includes an appendix arguing that people who haven't had an opportunity to hear and respond to the gospel can be saved anyway. That author writes, "God . . . would not be just if He held people accountable for that which they cannot do, and for knowledge they do not possess."[1] He goes on to suggest that God saves unevangelized people on the basis of a rudimentary faith in whatever meager revelation they might see and affirm in nature. In his view, then, people can be saved without ever trusting Christ as Savior or even knowing about him.

Such a broad view of salvation isn't even Protestant in any historic sense. If we allow for the possibility that responsible adult sinners can be saved without even knowing Christ,[2] then we are saying in effect that something other than faith in Christ may be instrumental for justification. That view implicitly abandons the Reformation principle of *sola fide*—faith as the sole instrument of justification. Moreover, it explicitly relinquishes the principle of *solus Christus*—Christ as the only object of the sinner's hope for salvation.

Worst of all, such a view isn't biblical. It makes the truth about Christ, and personal knowledge of him, optional. It suggests that God has an alternate plan for saving people, while allowing them to remain completely in the dark about Christ—as if God might begin the process of saving someone, but be thwarted in the attempt before the person has an opportunity to hear the gospel.

Scripture clearly teaches that God effectually calls those whom he chooses for salvation. Paul wrote, "Whom He predestined, these He also called; whom He called, these He also justified; and whom He justified, these He also glorified" (Rom. 8:30). In John 6:37, Jesus said, "All that the Father gives Me will come to Me, and the one who comes to Me I will by no means cast out." Whatever God begins, he finishes. There are no spiritual abortions. There is no such thing as someone who begins to respond to the light of revelation, but dies before receiving the message of the gospel.

Those whom God calls, he calls through the gospel, and he calls them unto belief in the truth. The apostle Paul says so explicitly: "God from the beginning chose you for salvation through sanctification by the Spirit *and belief in the truth,* to which *He called you by our gospel,* for the obtaining of the glory of our Lord Jesus Christ" (2 Thess. 2:13–14). Jesus said, "My sheep hear My voice, and I know them, and they follow Me" (John 10:27). He taught that belief in him is absolutely essential for salvation: "If you do not believe that I am He, you will die in your sins" (John 8:24). The context of that verse shows that he was speaking of his deity. In other words, he was demanding that people embrace him as God and make him the sole object of their trust and worship.

Virtually everyone in the evangelical movement fifty years ago understood that. It is what the true church of Christ has always believed and taught. The gospel itself is a message about *the exclusivity of Christ.* And the gospel must be preached to the ends of the earth, so that people who have never heard of Christ can be saved. That is the Christian mission. It is our mandate from the Lord himself: "Go into all the world and preach the gospel to every creature" (Mark 16:15). True Christians have always been compelled by the fact that if people don't hear the gospel, they cannot be saved. And if they are not saved, they will spend eternity in hell under the judgment of God.

By contrast, the author of the book I have been citing constructs an elaborate theory in which he suggests that Christ's death on the cross erased the universal guilt of original sin. "People no longer go to hell because of what Adam did," he writes. "They go to hell for what *they* do. God took care of Adam's sin on the cross. He paid for original sin."[3] Therefore, according to that author, only one sin is actually damnable: a deliberate, conscious rejection of God's revealed truth—specifically, a rejection of the way of salvation. He writes,

"The only thing God will not tolerate is people who willingly suppress His truth and reject His salvation."[4] Apparently, he is convinced that many people who have never even heard the name of Jesus Christ will be in heaven because they have not consciously rejected him.

What has convinced that author that people can be saved apart from the gospel? In his words, "The premise is this: God's invitation to all people to respond in faith assumes that those who have been invited have the capacity to respond. To put it another way, God's command to believe is only applicable to those who can heed it."[5]

But Scripture plainly says that *no one* can respond in faith by his or her own power. Jesus said, "No one can come to Me unless the Father who sent Me draws him" (John 6:44). Paul wrote, "The carnal mind is enmity against God; for it is not subject to the law of God, *nor indeed can be*. So then, those who are in the flesh *cannot* please God" (Rom. 8:7–8). In other words, Scripture is full of commandments that sinful people have absolutely no capacity to fulfill, starting with the first and great commandment ("Love the LORD your God with all your heart, with all your soul, and with all your mind"—Matt. 22:37) and culminating with Jesus' summary command in the Sermon on the Mount: "Be perfect, just as your Father in heaven is perfect" (Matt. 5:48).

So it is a serious mistake to imagine that God's command to believe assumes that sinners have the ability to do so in their own power or by their own "free will."

Furthermore, the author in question is convinced that some who have no access to the gospel are sincerely seeking God anyway, and that God is obliged to save them apart from the gospel. He says, "When it comes to salvation, God always makes a way for those who seek Him."[6] Here he cites Hebrews 11:6 and Jeremiah 29:13, and suggests that when people respond to what they know about God and begin seeking him, it is God's responsibility to give them more light. But if circumstances make that impossible, or if the persons in question die before receiving the gospel, God must save them on the basis of their "faith" in whatever truth they have deduced from the light of nature.

The problem with that view is that no one does seek God. Scripture is explicit: "There is none who seeks after God. They have all gone out of the way; they have together become unprofitable; there is none who does good, *no, not one*" (Rom. 3:11–12). People come to Christ only when God draws them. No one seeks God apart from his own gracious enablement. That is why Jesus said, "No one can come to Me unless it has been granted to him by My Father" (John 6:65; cf. v. 44).

Furthermore, all people are already guilty of suppressing the light of divine truth in nature. That is the whole point of Romans 1:18–32. Humanity as a whole, including every person individually, has suppressed the truth about God revealed in his creation and has disobeyed what is known from nature to be true. Their own consciences bear witness to this (Rom. 2:15). In fact, whether they will admit it or not, all non-Christians hate the God of Scripture and are spiritually dead. They are incapable of obeying him or earning his favor for salvation by anything they do (Rom. 8:7–8; Eph. 2:1–3). Therefore, under any theology that depends on the sinner's own free will to initiate movement toward God, everyone would be eternally damned.

Moreover, if sinners could be saved without any knowledge of Christ, or if all they had to do was avoid any conscious, willful suppression of whatever truth they know, or if they could be saved by other means, as long as they do not deliberately reject Christ, then the best thing for Christians to do would be to keep the gospel to themselves, because it is a stumbling block and mere foolishness to the typical unbeliever who hears it (1 Cor. 1:22–23). Proclaiming the gospel would simply give people more difficult truth to be held accountable for, and thus increase the chances that they will be damned.

But Scripture teaches that people who are without the gospel are lost and condemned. "How then shall they call on Him in whom they have not believed? And how shall they believe in Him of whom they have not heard? And how shall they hear without a preacher? And how shall they preach unless they are sent? . . . So then faith comes by hearing, and hearing by the word of God" (Rom. 10:14–17).

It is absolutely critical that the people of the world hear the gospel of Jesus Christ in order for them to be saved. Not only must they hear it, but they must also understand it, believe it, and embrace Christ for themselves. He is their only hope for salvation, and the gospel is the only saving truth about him.

Clearly, Christ is the only Savior, and only by explicit faith in him can anyone be saved. Let's examine a few passages of Scripture that make that point even clearer.

GENESIS 3

The place to start is the book of Genesis, beginning with the creation and fall of Adam. If anyone ever had a clear knowledge of God from creation, it was Adam. If any sinner might have found a way of salvation without any special revelation from God, Adam and Eve ought to have been able to do it. They knew God, before they fell, through face-to-face fellowship with him in the Garden. They lived in a perfect environment that was not at all tainted with the curse of sin, and they had a perfect relationship with the Creator.

Even in that perfect environment, however, they could not discover everything they needed to know. Even though their minds were as perfect as human minds could be, and their rational faculties were unspoiled by the effects of sin, there were essential spiritual principles they needed to know that lay outside the scope of human reason. That is why God spoke and gave them instructions. They were to be fruitful and multiply (Gen. 1:28). They could eat freely of the fruit of any tree, except one (2:16–17). Those things they knew only because God told them. In other words, they needed special revelation in order to understand the way of life.

Robert Morey writes:

> Adam was not created to be the Origin of truth, justice, morals, meaning and beauty. The Creator assumed the form of a man and walk[ed] with man in the Garden in the cool of the day. He would call Adam and Eve to come to him. They dropped whatever they were doing and walked and talked with the Son of God. They had so many questions and He had all the answers.
>
> These daily sessions were Special Revelation. God told man why He created him and what he was to do in the Garden. He revealed to man what he could and could not eat. In other words, God was the Origin or Source of truth, justice, morals, meaning and beauty. Man's responsibility was to receive what God revealed. Man was not the Origin but the receiver of truth.[7]

Certainly, some truths about God were evident in creation. A rudimentary moral sense was inherent in their conscience, so Adam and Eve knew that God was righteous. They could see some of his attributes—tokens of his power and glory—on display in creation. But all of that was not sufficient to show them the way of life. They still needed truth through special revelation.

After Adam and Eve fell, how could they stand in God's presence? They intuitively knew that they had sinned and needed a covering. For the first time ever, they sensed shame in their own nakedness ("The eyes of both of them were opened, and they knew that they were naked," Gen. 3:7). But even with all their knowledge of God, they were unable to devise an adequate covering on their own. With their superior minds, with all the light of nature they had access to, and even with their vast knowledge of God and his character gleaned from face-to-face walks with him, they did not know how to make themselves fit to stand before him after they had sinned. Scripture says, "They sewed fig leaves together and made themselves coverings" (v. 7).

Their efforts, like all human efforts to cover sin, were inadequate. So God himself killed an animal and fashioned clothing for them from an animal skin. It was a graphic symbol that showed what Scripture would later explicitly reveal: "Without shedding of blood there is no remission [of sin]" (Heb. 9:22). "It is the blood that makes atonement for the soul" (Lev. 17:11). The death of a perfect substitute is the price of an adequate covering for sin.

Furthermore, after pronouncing the curse that resulted from their sin, God gave them a promise of salvation. He said to the serpent, "I will put enmity between you and the woman, and between your seed and her Seed; He shall bruise your head, and you shall bruise His heel" (Gen. 3:15). That verse is known as the *protoevangelium*—the first hint of the

159

gospel. It was a promise that the woman's Seed, Christ, would crush the serpent, Satan, and thereby destroy his evil work forever (cf. Heb. 2:14). It gave them reason to hope and an object for their hope—Christ alone. Thus, the principle of *solus Christus* is rooted in the earliest promise of salvation.

Adam and Eve could not have found such hope apart from the divinely revealed promise. They could never have discerned the way of salvation from nature alone. Nor can people today. The special revelation of Scripture—the gospel message in particular—is absolutely essential.

The Old Testament is filled with revealed truth that is necessary for life and godliness. It outlines humanity's specific duties before God. It records the history of God's dealings with his people. And running through it all is the echo of God's promise of a Deliverer—the Messiah (Christ)—who would save his people from their sins (e.g., Gen. 49:10; Num. 24:17–19; Deut. 18:15, 18–19; Isa. 9:6–7; Mic. 5:2). Thus, Christ was the ultimate object of faith even for Old Testament believers. That is why Jesus himself said, "If you believed Moses, you would believe Me; for he wrote about Me" (John 5:46).

Faith in those promises was essential to the salvation of Old Testament saints (cf. John 8:56). Without the promises themselves and the message they conveyed, the way of salvation would have remained unknown, and people could not have discovered it by any natural means. "How shall they believe in Him of whom they have not heard?" (Rom. 10:14).

ROMANS 1

In the New Testament, Romans 1:18–23 outlines the fate of those whose only knowledge of spiritual truth comes from natural revelation. This is a definitive passage, with far-reaching implications. This is the biblical view of fallen humanity. It is a foundational passage for biblical anthropology. I already referred to this passage above. Now let's look at it carefully.

The apostle Paul writes:

> For the wrath of God is revealed from heaven against all ungodliness and unrighteousness of men, who suppress the truth in unrighteousness, because what may be known of God is manifest in them, for God has shown it to them. For since the creation of the world His invisible attributes are clearly seen, being understood by the things that are made, even His eternal power and Godhead, so that they are without excuse, because, although they knew God, they did not glorify Him as God, nor were thankful, but became futile in their thoughts, and their foolish hearts were darkened. Professing to be wise, they became fools, and changed the glory of the incorruptible God into an image made like corruptible man—and birds and four-footed animals and creeping things. (Rom. 1:18–23)

That passage states clearly that all people have some knowledge of God. Such knowledge is inherent in the mind of every human—it is "manifest in them" (v. 19). Knowledge of God is also manifest in the rest of creation as we observe what God has made (v. 20). Anyone can look at the diversity of creation and see that God must have an immense mind. He is clearly a God of order, beauty, power, and complexity. Those things are "clearly seen." People in effect have to commit intellectual suicide in order to deny that there is a Cause for the effect of the universe—a Creator. That's why there is enough truth in nature to condemn humanity and leave people without excuse (v. 20). But is it enough to save them?

No, it is not. The truth of nature leads no one to God. In the first place, there is not enough truth in nature to reveal the way of salvation. The promises of Christ and the truth about him that is essential to the gospel cannot be discerned naturally by human reason. If Adam and Eve in their unfallen state needed special revelation to explain their duties, and if in their early fallen state they were utterly dependent on special revelation to show them the way of salvation, how much more do we need God's Word to point us to Christ?

In the second place, the effects of sin on the human mind have made it impossible for fallen humanity to discover the way to God in nature. Sin causes all sinners to suppress the truth in unrighteousness (v. 18). Every sinner is so thoroughly wicked, so completely depraved, so vile in nature, that his or her depravity negates the possibility of finding God through the power of rational thought and nature alone. Instead, the sinner suppresses the truth. He dishonors the Creator. He can do nothing else on his own.

Beginning in verse 21, the apostle Paul traces the inevitable decline of the human mind. Although the knowledge of God is obvious all around, all people, left to their own devices, refuse to honor the Creator. They will not be thankful for the many tokens of his goodness and care. They turn away from the true God. They become futile in their thoughts, and their foolish hearts are darkened (v. 21). That is the genesis of all false religion. People come up with stupid ideas that aren't true—false religions, the doctrine of evolution, or vain philosophies. They invent empty ideas, and they are left in the darkness of their own imaginations.

People in such a state often profess to be wise, but they are fools (v. 22). Some give themselves academic degrees or put on royal garb, religious robes, cone hats, or other costumes and parade around as if they were great religious wise men. Others join monasteries, assume ascetic lifestyles, and withdraw from the world with a great show of austerity. Still others invent their own religions, pretend to have discovered ultimate truth within themselves, and in essence declare themselves gods. The rest renounce all forms of religion and insist that atheism, agnosticism, or humanism is the highest form of wisdom. They worship at the shrine of their own impotent rationalism. All of them are fools. The Greek word that speaks of becoming fools in verse 22 is the verb *mōrainō*—from the same root as the English word *moron*.

But it doesn't stop there. Verse 23 describes how they exchange the glory of the incorruptible God for images in the form of humans, birds, four-footed animals, snakes, and bugs. They make their own gods out of other created things. That's where human wisdom ends up whenever sinners seek something to worship without benefit of God's special revelation. That is the inevitable course of all "natural theology."

Why? Because Scripture says that sinners are dead in trespasses and sins (Eph. 2:1). They are not alive to God. They are not alive to truth. In their deadness, they suppress the truth that they otherwise might see. Righteousness is abandoned. And in its place come false religious systems, empty philosophies, and debauchery of the worst sort.

Can such a course lead someone to salvation? To ask the question is to answer it. The end of human philosophy and human religion is not salvation, but "the wrath of God" (v. 18).

That's the whole point of this passage. The natural man, with his natural theology unaided by special revelation, ends up subject to divine judgment. You can examine any false religion or philosophy as carefully as you like, and you will not discover the saving grace of God. The end of all such things is divine wrath. No matter what twisted remnants of God's moral and ethical code you might discover in this or that false religion, it is not saving truth. It can redeem no one. It is not "good." In fact, man-made religion is the *worst* evil that humanity has ever devised. And it is the predictable end to which human reason, apart from divine revelation, invariably leads. Religion without Christ is a damning delusion.

Still, many professing Christians who hold a broader view of salvation will claim that such people *are* saved by Christ—but without knowing him explicitly. One author who helped pioneer this way of thinking wrote, "The good and *bona fide* Hindu is saved by Christ and not by Hinduism, but it is through the sacraments of Hinduism, through the message of morality and good life, through the *Mysterion* that comes down to him through Hinduism, that Christ saves the Hindu normally."[8]

A similar view is expressed by Peter Kreeft in his book *Ecumenical Jihad.* He suggests that "even atheists and agnostics, if they are of good will . . . can be called 'anonymous Christians.' "[9] Amazingly, Kreeft contends that the messages of Confucius, Buddha, and Mohammed do not conflict with the essential message of Christianity. In fact, one chapter of his book is devoted to a lengthy description of Kreeft's vision of heaven. He claims that Confucius, Buddha, and Mohammed are there right along with Moses.

Still more disturbing is this: the book jacket carries endorsements by a couple of key evangelical leaders. One of them, a highly respected evangelical theologian, says, "Catholics, Protestants, and Orthodox alike need to ponder Peter Kreeft's vision of things. What if he is right?"

Clearly, evangelicals are already moving in that direction. The evangelical author of the book I referred to at the beginning of this chapter says, "A person can be saved without knowing Jesus' name, but not without Jesus' provision for sin."[10]

But can people be saved without expressly repenting of and abandoning false religion and human philosophy and consciously embracing Christ alone? Romans 1 is God's own diagnosis of the spiritual lostness of natural humanity. That passage makes clear that people on their own suppress the truth they have. Religion is of no benefit whatever to those who do not know the gospel of Christ. In fact, such people often become extremely religious, but their religion is only a descent into worse depravity; it is not an ascent to God. Its end is judgment, not salvation. It leads to divine wrath, not grace. It is a broad road that leads to destruction, away from Christ. It is not, and never can be, a pathway to the Savior.

1 CORINTHIANS 1

The opening chapter of Paul's first epistle to the Corinthians includes a passage that is a partner with Romans 1. Paul writes, "For the message of the cross is foolishness to those who are perishing" (v. 18). Apart from Christ, natural religion not only causes people to become fools (Rom. 1:22), but also deludes them into thinking that the truth is foolish.

In contrast, "to us who are being saved [the message of the cross] is the power of God" (1 Cor. 1:18). This is precisely where Paul launches his discussion of humanity's descent in Romans 1: The gospel "is the power of God to salvation [only] for everyone who believes" (v. 16).

Notice another parallel between Romans 1 and 1 Corinthians 1. As we saw in Romans 1, divine wrath is the ultimate end of human rationalism. Here in 1 Corinthians 1:19, Paul says (blending prophecies from Isaiah 19:3 and 29:14), "For it is written: 'I will destroy the wisdom of the wise, and bring to nothing the understanding of the prudent.'" God threatens to destroy those who achieve religious wisdom, who rise to the highest level of rational human understanding. This echoes the pronouncement of wrath in Romans 1:18. Rather than rewarding the highest human wisdom, God condemns it. He will bring it to nothing.

Verse 20 is a powerful challenge to human "goodness": "Where is the wise? Where is the scribe? Where is the disputer of this age? Has not God made foolish the wisdom of this world?" God is going to bring to nothing the wisest of the wise, the elite religious leaders ("the scribe"), the best dialecticians in the world. That is true of religious leaders, world rulers, popular politicians, philosophical and scientific geniuses, authors, artists, academic leaders, and every other kind of human prodigy. All their wisdom, their moral discipline, and their finest accomplishments will not earn them salvation. Apart from Christ, they are lost.

Paul's point is clear, and it flatly refutes the notion that anyone can find salvation on his or her own, without the light of the gospel. Only the message of the cross can save; everything else is foolish (v. 20)—*mōros,* moronic. "For since, in the wisdom of God, the world through wisdom did not know God, it pleased God through the foolishness (*mōria*) of the message preached to save those who believe" (v. 21).

There is only one way to be saved. Human wisdom can't get you there; man-made religion won't do it, either. God's chosen means of redeeming people is "through the foolishness of the message preached." What message? The message about Christ. Specifically, the good news of Christ's death and res-

166

urrection. There is no alternative plan of salvation. That is why it is essential that we preach the gospel to every creature.

By the way, "those who believe" are not any people who believe just anything. They believe in *Christ*. Their faith is a gift from God.

Satan hasn't changed since his first appearance in the Garden of Eden. He still questions the word of God. He sows doubt. He disputes the necessity of the gospel. "You don't really think people cannot be saved without the gospel, do you? Trust your own reason." Sadly, that is precisely what many modern evangelicals have done. And when they decide that the gospel is optional, they are following Satan.

As a matter of fact, aside from the wisdom revealed by God in the gospel, there is only one other kind of "wisdom." It is described in James 3:15, "This wisdom does not descend from above, but is earthly, sensual, demonic." It is not only wrong; it is not merely foolish; it is *demonic*.

People cannot get to God through any system of their own devising. You either come through Jesus Christ, or you don't get there. Even the wisest of the wise and the cleverest of the clever will be brought to nothing, apart from Christ. The world through its wisdom can know Satan, but cannot know God. Scripture makes that perfectly clear.

1 CORINTHIANS 2

Moving to chapter 2 of 1 Corinthians, we find Paul developing a similar theme. In verses 9–10, he says, quoting Isaiah, "'Eye has not seen, nor ear heard, nor have entered into the heart of man the things which God has prepared for those who love Him.' But God has revealed them to us through His

Spirit. For the Spirit searches all things, yes, the deep things of God."

Here's a simple principle: the things of God do not naturally penetrate the mind of fallen man. Sinners are morally and spiritually incapable of discovering the truth about God through the workings of their own minds. If we want to know what God thinks, if we want to know what is not empirically visible in creation, if we want to understand the saving truth about God—what his law demands, how we can be redeemed from the curse of the law, and how Christ perfectly fulfilled the law's demands on behalf of his people—then we are utterly dependent on the Spirit of God, working through the Word of God, to show us those things. Such thoughts do not naturally enter into anyone's mind.

Obviously, the Spirit of God knows the deep things of God, because the Spirit *is* God. He knows what we don't know. He "searches" those things, and so he knows them intimately, as only God himself can know.

Verse 11 introduces an analogy: "For what man knows the things of a man except the spirit of the man which is in him? Even so no one knows the things of God except the Spirit of God." You don't really know someone else's thoughts. Even in the closest of human relationships—spouses, identical twins, or a mother and her child—one person cannot truly know the thoughts of the other person. We don't really have telepathic access to others' minds. All we can know is what is manifest through words and behavior. Besides God, who perfectly sees our heart (Ps. 139:1–4), the only person who truly and thoroughly knows a human thought is the man who has the thought.

So it is with God. His Spirit knows very well what is going on in the mind and heart of God, because the Spirit himself *is* God. He alone knows the "deep things." You and I have no means of discovering "the deep things" unless the Spirit of God makes them known to us by special revelation. After all, we cannot even know the mind of another human being. How could we ever hope to know the mind of God by our own devices?

But the Spirit of God has revealed the mind of God. He does not directly and immediately reveal fresh truth to the mind of every believer. Rather, he speaks to us through his Word—the Scripture. When Paul writes that "we have received, not the spirit of the world, but the Spirit who is from God, that we might know the things that have been freely given to us by God" (v. 12), he is specifically speaking of himself and the other apostles. This is a claim of inspiration. He is saying that the teaching of the apostles is a perfect, infallible revelation of the mind of the Spirit: "These things we also speak, not in words which man's wisdom teaches but which the Holy Spirit teaches" (v. 13). And that same revelation is inscripturated for us in the written Word of God.

I like the way the New American Standard Bible translates verse 13: ". . . which things we also speak, not in words taught by human wisdom, but in those taught by the Spirit, combining spiritual thoughts with spiritual words." That is what the human authors of Scripture did. They recorded spiritual thoughts, revealed to them by the Spirit of God, with spiritual words, also sovereignly chosen by the Spirit. And so in Scripture we have an infallible record of the Spirit's revelation.

We cannot know the deep things of God apart from that revelation. We cannot arrive at those truths by human reason alone. Such truths cannot be found in a scientific experiment. They cannot be discovered by observing creation. They are known only by the special revelation of the Holy Spirit.

But here's an amazing reality: fallen, unregenerate people are even blind to the explicit revelation of Scripture. Apart from the illuminating work of the Holy Spirit, they cannot grasp its truths. Verse 14 makes the point inescapable: "But the natural man does not receive the things of the Spirit of God, for they are foolishness to him; nor can he know them, because they are spiritually discerned."

A natural man, by his own intellectual prowess, simply cannot know the things of the Spirit of God—even when the words of Scripture are staring him right in the face. He can't process the truth. He has no spiritual capacity to comprehend spiritual things. To him, they are foolishness. What does religion, apart from the gospel of Jesus Christ, accomplish in bringing people to God? Nothing. It is counterproductive. The best that human wisdom can produce is sophisticated ignorance—polished, elegant, but demonic folly.

CONCLUSION

One author I read said he believes that unevangelized people will fare all right in the judgment, because when they die, whatever they don't know in this earthly life will get straightened out in heaven. He has evidently concluded that God would be unjust not to give everyone a second chance after this life is over. But Scripture says nothing like that. Rather, "it is appointed for men to die once, but after this the judgment" (Heb. 9:27).

That is why we must continue to proclaim Christ to every creature. He is the only Savior. Faith in him is the only instrument of justification. The gospel is the only hope of the world. *Solus Christus* is the clear teaching of the Bible.

Natural theology reduces people to ignorant idol worshipers, engaged with demons and headed for divine judgment. Natural revelation is sufficient to damn, but not to save. It leaves sinners without excuse, but not without condemnation. Apart from the truth of Christ, and explicit faith in him alone, no one can be saved.

Our duty as responsible Christians is therefore clear: "Go into all the world and preach the gospel to every creature" (Mark 16:15). Proclaim "Jesus Christ and Him crucified" (1 Cor. 2:2). As Christ himself prayed on the night of his betrayal, "This is eternal life, that they may know You, the only true God, and Jesus Christ whom You have sent" (John 17:3).

9

PERSEVERANCE OF
THE SAINTS

JAY E. ADAMS

Throughout his writings, John Calvin sounded the note of certainty. His certainty had a powerful influence on the Reformation. He was deeply concerned that believers should know the certainty of their salvation. Rome's ceremonialism and system of merit had utterly obscured the biblical truth that in this life men can know that they will spend eternity in the presence of God. One reason for this flawed understanding of God's truth was the belief that those once saved could again be lost. Calvin wanted to remove the fear of losing salvation, which alone caused many to adhere to Romanist error. Rather, he wanted believers to know that their salvation was assured in Christ, resulting in confidence and love in place of fear.

The scriptural doctrine of the perseverance of the saints, which Calvin strongly championed, was the key to maintaining one's certainty of salvation. I am delighted to reexamine the biblical evidence for the cheerful and soul-warming teaching of the perseverance of the saints, especially at the present time, when in some "evangelical" circles all of the doctrines established at the Reformation are considered up for grabs.

WHAT PETER HAD TO SAY

Perhaps the clearest statement of the doctrine of perseverance is found in 1 Peter 1:3–5:[1]

> Let us praise the God and Father of our Lord Jesus Christ, Who according to His great mercy regenerated us for a living hope through the resurrection of Jesus Christ from the dead, for an incorruptible, unspotted and unfading inheritance that has been kept in the heavens for you who are guarded by God's power through faith for a salvation that is ready to be revealed in the last time.

NOTHING CAN GO WRONG WITH THE INHERITANCE

Peter makes it clear that the heavenly inheritance of the saints is secure. There is nothing that can destroy or even mar it, because it is "incorruptible, unspotted and unfading." Earthly things, as Jesus pointed out, have the very opposite characteristics: "moth and rust can ruin them" (Matt. 6:19). But the heavenly inheritance is of a nature that cannot be so affected. Being a spiritual inheritance, in God's spiritual realm, it is entirely out of the reach of such things. So there is no doubt about the integrity of the salvation that Jesus purchased for his own. Moreover, this inheritance, as Peter says, is "kept" in the heavens. It is a trust that God has committed into his own hands for safekeeping. If the almighty preserving power of God is being exerted to protect it, then we can be absolutely certain that nothing can go wrong with our future inheritance.

NOTHING CAN GO WRONG WITH THE HEIR

But those who believe that people once saved may lose their salvation often point to the vulnerability of the believer himself. The believer, they think, is the weak link in the chain. "Of course," they say, "no one can snatch him from God's hand, but he can wander and fall from grace on his own." But Peter will have nothing to do with this notion. He knows of no weak link. His words make it perfectly clear that God has covered all the bases. He assures his readers that just as nothing can go wrong with the inheritance, so also can nothing go wrong with the heir. He too is "guarded by God's power," and there is no power greater than God's—least of all the power of a believer to tear himself loose from God's safekeeping.

Moreover, as some might fail to notice, Peter makes it absolutely plain that the guarding takes place "through faith." That can mean nothing else than that the faith which saves (originally a gift from God, according to Eph. 2:8–9) is so nurtured and cared for by the Spirit of God that no genuine believer ever does apostatize. The phrase "through faith" is telling for the argument, since it is a supposed loss of faith that is the thrust of the attack by those who believe in the possibility of losing salvation. It is here that they believe the weak link is to be found. But Peter parries their thrust by saying that it is precisely through—by means of—faith that God preserves the believer. God's safekeeping "power" works through the faith of the believer. In other words, it is precisely because the power of God is manifested in preserving the Christian's faith that he can be assured of never losing his salvation.

BUT THAT'S NOT ALL

The perseverance of believers in the faith is also clearly taught in John 17, a powerful passage that is often misinterpreted. Here we are privileged to listen in on what has been called the High Priestly Prayer of Christ. In it, he speaks of believers becoming "one" so that "the world may believe that You sent Me" (v. 21). This prayer has been consistently understood by liberals (and, sadly, of late by conservatives as well) as teaching that organic union (or, at least, corporate expressions of unity) among Christians will lead the world to believe in Christ. If that were true, then Jesus' prayer has never been answered in the affirmative. Indeed, it could only be declared an utter failure! From the beginning, there have been strife and division among Christians, as the New Testament itself so plainly testifies. And church history records an unending stream of the same, flowing up until the present. But, of course, we must maintain that Christ's prayer for unity has not failed. How, then, do we explain the failure of churches to unite? The fact is that he prayed for nothing of the sort.

WHAT THE PRAYER WAS ALL ABOUT

For what then did Jesus pray? Surely he asked the Father that his followers might become one, didn't he? Yes, he did.

But the unity for which he prayed was not a horizontal unity among men; rather, he prayed for a vertical unity with himself, as indeed he is one with the Father. That truth is what many have failed to understand.

The entire prayer is a prayer that genuine believers may not be "destroyed" as Judas was (v. 12). Now that he was about to leave his own, he prayed that God would continue to "guard" them, just as he had previously "kept" them under his watchful care (v. 12). And he prayed not only for the apostles, but also for those who would come to believe under their preaching (v. 20). The kind of guarding that Jesus had in mind is explained in verse 21: ". . . that all may be one just as You, Father, are one with Me and I with You; that they too may be one with Us, so that the world may believe that You sent Me."

AN INSEPARABLE UNITY

The unity involved in these words is a unity with the Father and the Son, a unity that is as inseparable as that which these members of the Trinity enjoy! And in answer to his Son's prayer, God continues to bring disciples into such union with Jesus and himself, so that they are "guarded" from anything that might destroy them (vv. 12, 20–21). The world believed when, in the face of great persecution, true Christians refused to abandon their faith. The world could not fail to see that there was something different about them. Many came over to the faith when they saw that neither flame nor rack nor wild beasts could separate them from their love for God (and his love for them: cf. Rom. 8:38–39). They recognized that something beyond mere human grit filled the hearts of the martyrs who endured to the end. That something was the Father's answer to Jesus' prayer!

AND THAT'S NOT ALL, EITHER!

It is not difficult to understand the Romans syllogism of security, as I like to call it. Here it is:

- God's gifts and calling are not recalled (Rom. 11:29).
- God's gift is eternal life by Christ Jesus our Lord (Rom. 5:23).
- Therefore, God never recalls the gift of eternal life.

And you can run through it again, this time emphasizing the calling of God:

- God's gifts and calling are not recalled (Rom. 11:29).
- God's loved ones are called to be saints (Rom. 1:7).
- Therefore, God never recalls the calling to be a saint.

Nothing could be simpler. Paul is saying that God is no "Indian giver" (an expression that the politically incorrect still find useful). He doesn't make a promise, and then change his mind. He never hands us something with one hand, only to take it back with the other. He would never give eternal life to a person, and then later kill him spiritually. Eternal life is just that—life that lasts eternally in God's presence. God is true to his word. The certainty that Calvin taught was nothing new; it was first taught by Jesus, and then by Peter and Paul!

Add one more proof from Romans—the chain of certainty found in Romans 8:30: "And those whom He foreordained He also called, and those whom He called He also justified, and those whom He justified He also glorified." There is no weak link in the chain! It moves inexorably from foreordination to glorification.[2] The several declarations given by Paul are tied together in such a way that they are not subject to interruptions or alterations.

HOW ABOUT APOSTASY?

When, for instance, preachers from the heretical denomination called the Churches of Christ[3] speak of "the possibility of apostasy," they mean that those who were once truly saved may leave the faith, lose their salvation, and turn against the Lord Jesus Christ. Plainly, the Bible speaks about apostasy, but that is not what it means by the word. A very important verse that makes the truth about apostasy clear is 1 John 2:19: "They went out from us, but they weren't of us; because if they had been of us, they would have remained with us. But this happened that it might appear that all aren't of us."

In this verse, John is addressing the fact that certain Gnostic teachers who had been in the fold had left and were now teaching their heresy. Previously, they seemed to be true Christians, because there was no outward indication of their heretical belief. But their false views of the nature of Christ solidified and came to the fore, and they found that they could no longer fellowship with genuine Christians. So they apostatized, and denied that Christ died for our sins.[4]

In this verse, two important facts emerge. First, those who apostatized were never true believers. John says that by leaving they made it clear that this was so ("they weren't of us"). Indeed, while they had at one time been a part of the visible church, they had never belonged to the invisible church. Their profession of faith was false. This problem of a false profession of faith in Jesus Christ, which we so often encounter in our churches today, was also a problem in apostolic times. Those who teach that believers may apostatize from the church disregard John's plain explanation of the facts. We must not do so. Instead, we must maintain that those who denounce the faith never had true faith in the first place. They may have been among believers, but they were not of them. Otherwise, as John says, they would not have failed to persevere with them.

Second, note the corollary: John affirms that "if they had been of us, they would have remained with us." True believers remain in the faith and in the church! They endure to the end. It is certainly possible for a believer to defect for a time, but, like Peter or John Mark—who both had temporary lapses—in the end they will repent and return.

THE WRITER OF HEBREWS AGREES

In two places, the letter to the Hebrews addresses the problem in strong language. Consider the following:

> If we deliberately go on sinning after receiving the full knowledge of the truth, there no longer remains a sacrifice for sins, but only a fearful anticipation of judgment and the fury of fire that is going to consume God's adversaries. Somebody who has violated Moses' law dies on the testimony of two or three witnesses. How much worse do you think the punishment will be for anybody who tramples on God's Son, who has considered the covenantal blood that set him apart unclean, and who insults the Spirit of grace? (Heb. 10:26–29)

And:

> It is impossible to renew again to repentance those who have once been enlightened, who have tasted of the heavenly gift and have become sharers of the Holy Spirit, and

have tasted the goodness of God's Word and the miracles of the coming age, if they fall away, because they themselves crucify God's Son all over again and publicly disgrace Him. Now ground that drinks up the rain that frequently waters it and bears vegetation that is useful to those who farm it receives God's blessing, but ground that bears thorns and thistles is worthless, and is close to being cursed and finally burned. Even though we speak this way, dear friends, we have been convinced of better things about you—things that are true of those who have salvation. (Heb. 6:4–9)

Throughout the book of Hebrews, the writer shows a concern that his readers might "drift" from the truth in the face of persecution (Heb. 2:1; 12:4). This concern about those who might "fall away" leads him to warn them of the fearful eventualities that will come to those who do. As a result, the book is replete with both warnings and encouragements.

While he knew that true believers would not repudiate their Savior, the writer recognized the possibility that some among his readers might not be genuine Christians after all. So he described the way in which people may become a part of the body of Christ, participating in all of God's wonderful benefits that are provided for the life of the church, but eventually turn their backs on everything that they have experienced. There would be no way to renew them to a genuine profession of faith, he says, because there is only one true message—the very one that they would have rejected. So he describes how great a dishonor to Christ it would be for one to have heard, tasted, and rejected the gospel, and how terrible the consequences would be.

But, as he describes the situation in terms of an example,

he seems to conclude that his readers' faith is genuine—at least the faith of most of those to whom he is writing. The example is that of the rain watering the ground. The very same rain (teaching, Christian fellowship, etc.) falls on two patches of ground. One produces fruit; the other produces thorns and thistles. The first result refers to those who believe and persevere; the latter refers to those who do not. Then, applying that example to his readers, he declares: "We have been convinced of better things about you—things that are true of those who have salvation." Here the writer says that those who have salvation do not fall away. They do not apostatize.

GOD IS A GOOD FATHER

To teach that a person once saved may be lost is to impugn the fatherhood of God. It is to say that he so poorly raises his children that many become delinquents who "drop out" or must be disowned by him. But the Bible teaches otherwise. Hebrews says that the Lord "disciplines" each of his children in order to bring them into line when they go the wrong ways; if they receive no discipline, the book teaches, they are illegitimate (Heb. 12:5–11). And the effect of such discipline, we are assured, is that "it yields the peaceful fruit of righteousness to those who have been trained by it" (v. 11). God disciplines all of his legitimate children, and God's discipline gets positive results![5]

God does not allow rebellious children to wander away from the family or become so incorrigible that he must put them out. Those members who leave, or are permanently put out of the church, as we have seen, are false professors.

THERE ARE PRACTICAL CONSEQUENCES

This is by no means a merely academic discussion. To believe that one can be saved and lost leads to several serious consequences. For instance, a young man who had been taught this unbiblical doctrine once told me that he had finally "given up." Since, as he had discovered, he could not "keep himself saved," but supposedly kept falling in and out of salvation, he had concluded that he might as well live it up for whatever pleasures he could enjoy here and now in this life. After all, he would never reach heaven! And, according to all indications, he was not using this description and explanation of his experience as an excuse.

THERE'S THE PROBLEM OF SIN

Now, not everyone comes to the same logical conclusions that that young man did. Perhaps they should—it would expose the poverty of the belief that one may lose his salvation. But all who espouse his view of things certainly recognize that it is a severe struggle to maintain it. That is to say, they agonize over their salvation. That is because, in the final analysis, retaining it depends on them—and they know their own frailty and sinful propensities.

Others in the camp avoid that struggle by denuding the biblical nature of sin. For those who believe that they maintain their salvation by refraining from sin (either wholly or to a large extent), much of their sin becomes something less than sin. In order to qualify for a place in heaven by living up to whatever standard they set (the standard differs from group to group and person to person), much that Reformed people understand to be sin they call mistakes, errors, immaturity, and the like. Sin for them becomes something other and something less than sin.

A DETRIMENT TO SERVICE

For those sincere persons who have not settled the struggle with their sin by calling it something else, agonizing over whether or not one might lose his salvation in the end becomes debilitating. There is so much focus on the peril to oneself that such sincere (but sadly deceived) Christians have little time to devote to personal growth or to helping others. The doctrine does not turn out scholarly teachers, preachers of depth in the Word, or persons who spend their lives ministering to the saints or evangelizing the lost. Good intentions about such matters may arise within hearts, and valiant attempts may be made, but the fear of losing one's salvation demands a focus on oneself that dominates all they do. Much time spent in prayer about one's condition, in self-examination and introspection, cannot but consume many valuable hours. The practical, negative consequences of this false doctrine upon the Christian life are major.

PERSEVERANCE IS THE KEY

If you have been taught the once-saved-always-saved doctrine, you may think that there is no difference between that teaching and the doctrine of the perseverance of the saints. But there is. While it is certainly true that those who are once saved will always be saved, the concept of the perseverance of

184

the saints encompasses a truth that is rarely emphasized by people who teach the once-saved-always-saved view. That missing emphasis—which is of great importance—is the fact that a person is saved through perseverance, not apart from it.

The once-saved-always-saved view may lead those who hold it into quietistic thinking. That is to say, they may think that they have little or no part to play in maintaining their salvation. God does it all for them and instead of them. While a person is not saved by works (as Romanists believe)—nor does he remain saved by works (as the Churches of Christ believe)—God saves only those who persevere in the faith. That perseverance is the result of the work of the Spirit in their hearts, but, nevertheless, it is a work that enables them to keep on believing, as Peter says. God does not believe for them. They are "guarded" through faith.

In John 15, we read about the sanctification that is necessary for a believer to be saved.[6] A so-called "abiding" condition, which some Higher Life people take to mean a special sort of holiness, is not taught in the passage. That idea distorts the apostle's teaching. The Greek word *menō,* which the King James Version translates "abide," means "remain, continue, stay." It does not refer to some special state of "resting" in Christ that only super saints achieve. Rather, this abiding is equivalent to persevering in the faith. And it is true not of a select few, or of the apostles only, but of all Christians. Indeed, not only is persevering in one's faith in Christ necessary for bearing "much fruit," as the passage teaches, but also for salvation. Unless one remains in the vine, "he is thrown outside like a branch and withers" and, eventually, will be burned up (v. 6)! Jesus, therefore, commands, "Stay [or remain] in My love" (v. 9). The apostles—and all other believers—must persevere in their faith or be cast aside like a branch broken off the vine. Christ, the Vine, requires every professed Christian to remain in him by genuine faith, or eventually be thrown into the fire. So perseverance is the result of true faith, nourished and maintained by the Spirit. But the believer himself must continue to exercise it. He may never sit back and say, "I'm saved, I may do as I please, since I can never be lost."

To think that way indicates either that he has received very faulty teaching or that he never was a believer in the first place. No one, truly converted, can think that way for very long, if at all. True Spirit-given and Spirit-nourished faith leads to biblical thinking. A professed Christian must persevere—continue, remain, stay—in the Vine. Jesus spoke not only of remaining in him, but also of his "words" remaining in the believer (v. 7). Moreover, in verse 14 he said, "You are My friends if you do what I command you." After justification, by means of divinely guarded faith, one remains in salvation by the work of the Spirit, who, through that faith, enables him to continue obeying Jesus' words and commandments. That is perseverance.

This precious doctrine of the perseverance of the saints, coming down to us from the Reformation, must be preserved at all costs. We may neither abandon it nor compromise with those who would do so. The certainty of salvation, which Calvin so dearly wished his congregation to know, and which he bequeathed to subsequent generations, must not be lost. Those who today advocate "open theology" and similar heresies spawned by Arminian thinking that exalts man and debases God, cannot hold to perseverance. But they must not be allowed to spread their beliefs far and wide in the church of Christ without rebuttal. Stand up for the biblical doctrine against the inroads of such teaching. God is sovereign and his work may not be countered so as to be effectively set aside by man. Behind a denial of the doctrine of perseverance is a belief in the autonomy of man. Autonomy—were it true—would destroy God's sovereignty. Let us thank God that he is sovereign, and act and teach accordingly. Part and parcel of upholding that doctrine of sovereignty is an untarnished belief in perseverance.

10

SOLI DEO GLORIA

R. C. SPROUL JR.

Images are often misleading. When we think of the great Reformers, we tend to think of them as a rather dour crowd. They're great for writing heavy theology, but you wouldn't necessarily want to invite them to a party, unless your idea of a party is spending time with the dour crowd. They were gifted with keen minds, but not with much flair. We think of them as somber men, without a creative bone in their collective body. That mental cliché, however, might tell us more about ourselves than it tells us about the Reformers. I'm afraid we might be confusing them with ourselves.

I remember years ago that certain creative types on Madison Avenue were lauded for their genius in coming up with this slogan: "I can't believe I ate the whole thing." I venture to guess that most readers of this book have no recollection of that slogan. And of those who do remember it, only recovering television addicts can recall the product advertised. (It was Alka-Seltzer.)

The Reformers faced an enormous challenge. They not only had to correct the theological heresies of Rome, but also had to convince the people that Rome was indeed guilty of abandoning the true faith. To make matters worse, the people were used to being kept in the dark in theological matters. It wasn't enough for the Reformers to be right. It wasn't even enough for them to be persuasive. First, they had to get the people to listen. They had to grab the attention of the man in the pew, and once they had it, they had to keep it. Rome had at its disposal all its bells and whistles, and, oftentimes, a very big stick. All that the Reformers had was a great deal of creativity.

We may forget what we were supposed to buy when we remember "I can't believe I ate the whole thing," yet almost five hundred years after the start of the Reformation, we remember and honor its slogans, the *sola*s. These little summaries have serious staying power, as do the five points of the Synod of Dort. Since the Remonstrants brought forth their remonstration in the Netherlands, Reformed theologians have arranged these pithy points in an artistic way—the acrostic TULIP—which not only helps us to remember them, but even reminds us of their native land.

That this book is built around the five *sola*s and the five points of Calvinism not only displays our theological convictions, but shows the creativity of our fathers. Each of these short phrases can be understood on its own. They carry heavy freight. And in so doing, there is ample opportunity to unpack that freight, to unfurl the banners of the Reformation and show forth the fullness of our convictions.

But what if we had to choose only one of these little slogans? What if we found it too tiresome to carry around all ten of these banners? With the five points, it has often been rightly affirmed that if you really understood only the first one, total depravity, and if you wanted to be logically consistent, you would have to affirm all five. This means that our friends who claim to be four-point Calvinists not only are missing a point, but are missing the point. They belong in the oxymoron hall of fame, along with jumbo shrimp and government aid. Each of the points highlights a particular facet of the sovereignty of God.

In like manner, the five *sola*s are truly one. But if we were forced to pick one that best subsumes all the others, it would no doubt be the last one, *soli Deo gloria,* "to God alone the glory." If we began here, rather than ending here, we would surely still end here. More than anything else, what distinguishes the Reformed faith from all others is that it strives to understand all things in such a way that God alone receives the glory.

On the other hand, there is no theological system, save perhaps modern theological liberalism, that would dare to complain about the Reformed faith, "The problem with you guys is that you are always trying to make sure that God gets all the glory. It would be a far better thing to pass it around." What sets Reformed theology apart from all other systems, then, is not its verbal commitment to the glory of God, but the fact that it succeeds where all others fail.

Calvin begins his *Institutes* with an interesting paradox. He points out that in order for us to understand who God is, we must understand something of who man is. But it is likewise true that in order for us to understand who man is, we need to understand who God is. The Westminster Confession

191

of Faith, on the other hand, begins its systematic approach to the teaching of Scripture with its doctrine of Scripture. But when the Westminster divines set about putting together that most basic formulation of the Reformed faith, the one that was designed to bring children and new converts into the faith, the Shorter Catechism, they began with the glory of God. Question 1 reads, "What is the chief end of man?" The answer is deceptively simple: "Man's chief end is to glorify God, and to enjoy him forever." Already we see an echo of Calvin's paradox. But it would be fruitful for us to make that echo resound more fully by asking this question: "What is the chief end of God?" Once again, the answer is deceptively simple: "God's chief end is to glorify God, and to enjoy him forever." Our theological system is built on the pursuit of God's glory for the simple reason that the God of that theology is consumed with the pursuit of that glory.

And while it is perhaps true that only some things will in the long run enjoy God, it is likewise true that the single, overarching purpose of all things is to glorify God. In the weekly Bible study that I teach, we have come up with something of a liturgy to help us remember this truth. You don't have to attend long to know that anytime I ask any question beginning with "Why," whatever proximate answers might apply, the ultimate answer is always "For God's glory." Why are you reading this book? For God's glory.

To understand this better, we need to take a brief foray into that field of philosophy known as teleology. Teleology is the study of purposes or ends. Every time we act, we do so because we are seeking a particular goal. But things get complicated because we never seek only one goal. We seek one goal because it serves another more fundamental goal. I, for instance, am writing this chapter right now because of a series of goals. I want to make my deadline. I want to make my deadline because I want to be a man of my word. I want to be a man of my word because God's law requires me to be such. I want to obey God's law because this brings honor to God. Finally, I want to glorify God.

Also, I want to help people understand the Reformed faith. I want people to understand the Reformed faith because I believe this will better equip them to glorify God. And finally, I want to glorify God.

There is also a third thread. I want to honor my father. I want to honor my father because I want to give honor to whom honor is due. And I want to give honor to whom honor is due because this is the calling of God. And God is glorified when we do this. Each of these three goals—meeting my deadline, teaching the Reformed faith, and honoring my father—serves that one final goal, showing forth the glory of God.

We find much the same pattern when we consider the greatest of all questions: Why did God create this universe? The Bible begins, in one sense, in something of a hurry. There isn't much prolegomena. "In the beginning God created the heavens and the earth." But why? There have been any number of suggestions posited over the years. Perhaps the most common one coming from our pulpits is dead wrong. God did not create the world out of a sense of loneliness. There was no loneliness before the Creation. God the Father, God the Son, and God the Holy Spirit enjoyed a unity and an intimacy so intense that these three persons constitute one substance. The persons of the Trinity lacked nothing. Each member was, and is, both infinitely loveable and infinitely loving. There was no want before the beginning.

We, of course, are used to acting out of our wants, our

lacks. God, on the other hand, acts out of his fullness. Medieval theologians called the problem of God's lacking a lack appropriately enough, the "full bucket" problem. God's eternal joy is as complete as a completely full bucket is full. So why did he create? For his glory. The solution to the problem is to understand that the creation exists to show forth the unfathomable glory of God. It is only when we see the universe as existing for our purposes that it seems too large. Instead, it exists for his glory, and so is just right.

The Scripture tells us this as David, under the inspiration of the Holy Spirit, writes:

> The heavens declare the glory of God; and the firmament shows His handiwork. Day unto day utters speech, and night unto night reveals knowledge. There is no speech nor language where their voice is not heard. Their line had gone out through all the earth, and their words to the end of the world. (Ps. 19:1–4)

Even here, however, we need to be careful. Too often we take a modernist approach to how God's glory is shown forth in the creation. We study his creation and find that if God had set the earth's axis one degree this way, we would all burn up. If he had set the earth's axis one degree the other way, we would all freeze. Or we look at the gravitational balance of the galaxy and marvel at the clockwork precision of the movement of the stars. Or we turn to smaller things, and are astounded and baffled by the precise engineering of subatomic particles. When we see how things work, as we think God's thoughts after him, we give him praise.

This is an utterly appropriate approach, but it misses something important. It misses the sovereignty of God. Because the Bible begins with "In the beginning God," because once there was God and nothing else, he did not come to the creation of the world as an engineer might. An engineer has to balance God's world of givens. He must take into account rates of heat transfer, tensile strength of various materials, magnetism, and gravity. God has no such constraints. He could have made the earth flat. He could have given the earth no orbit or an orbit in the shape of a five-pointed star. Oh, but wait, you say, that would mess up centrifugal force, wouldn't it? No, because God invented that too. He could have made a universe in which things stay in perfect balance precisely because of the five-pointed-star orbit of the earth.

In short, God did not order the universe as an engineer might. Yes, the universe shows forth his creativity. That creativity, however, is shown forth in the poetry, or in the dance, of the creation, not in the design of it. The stars do what they do to show forth the beauty of God, not his mechanical prowess. And, in like manner, the dance of the subatomic particles operates under the same principle. And, more profoundly still, the dance of the stars and the dance of the subatomic particles join together in one great proclamation of the glory of God.

All of the creation, then, is wrapped up in this final *sola, soli Deo gloria*. Here among the *sola*s we look beyond God's relationship to man and consider instead God's relationship to reality, to the creation. It is one grand stage, a display of the glory of God.

The creation, however, is not the end of the story of his glory, but rather the setting of the story. I've been to some pretty grand stages in my life—concert halls, summer stock theaters, Heinz Hall in Pittsburgh. But as grand as these palaces of performance might be, they do not stand on their own. They do not exist for their own grandeur, but to be suitable settings for the presentation of something far grander. In like manner, the creation is the theater of God's glory, in which the great story of his glory is presented. The name of that great story is History.

Everything in the universe happens for one ultimate purpose, to make manifest the glory of God. The Reformers understood this in a way that we too often miss. We find it easy to see how God's glory is manifested in our salvation. It is a great thing indeed that God so loved the world that he gave his only begotten Son, that whosoever believeth in him should not perish but have eternal life. But what happened between the giving of the Son and my believing is just historical bunk. And what happens between my believing and my receiving eternal life is all future bunk. Thinking about my future peace in eternity may offer me some comfort in the midst of this present hardship, but there is no real connection between what God has done for my soul and what goes on from day to day, right?

Not if *soli Deo gloria* moves beyond telling us how to live our lives in our current situation. To believe *soli Deo gloria,* "to God alone the glory," certainly contains the idea that all that we do as believers ought to serve that ultimate purpose of showing forth the glory of God. But it also describes all that has happened and all that will happen. It affirms that God's stage is all the universe, that it is all his, to show forth his glory. And history is the same. He is not just sovereign over "sacred" or "redemptive" history, but over all history. He is glorified not only in the redemption of sinners, but also in the damnation of sinners. Paul says as much in Romans 9:22–23, "What if God, wanting to show His wrath and to make His power known, endured with much longsuffering the vessels of wrath prepared for destruction, and that He might make known the riches of His glory on the vessels of mercy, which He had prepared beforehand for glory."

It's astounding how important little words can be. Note that Paul doesn't say that God shows his wrath so that he can show his mercy. Hell is not merely a backdrop against which God can display his mercy. Instead, Paul joins together these two ideas with an "and." God is glorified in showing forth his wrath and in showing forth his mercy. Now, history is not only the story of how God redeems a stubborn and rebellious people, but also the story of how he brings judgment against stubborn and rebellious people. Thus, even the reprobate, while they will not enjoy God forever, will serve to manifest his glory.

To put it another way, because all people fall into one of two categories—those who will glorify God by being the objects of his just wrath, and those who will glorify God by being the objects of his tender mercy—all people do indeed show forth the glory of God. Nothing is "off-stage" in all of history.

If you were to travel back in time eight hundred years, but stay put geographically, what would you find? Here in America, you would find people whose lives had been untouched by the gospel of Jesus Christ. You would see cultures so decadent that it would make your head spin. God, at that point, had sent no missionaries to them. What could this possibly have to do with the glory of God? Everything. For, as we remember, the creation itself speaks of the glory of God. And yet, because those native Americans, like us, were sinners, they suppressed this truth, revealed through creation, in unrighteousness. They exchanged the truth for a lie, and worshiped the creature rather than the Creator. And because they were doing this, they were heaping up wrath against themselves, which

God would pour out on them at the appointed hour. They were still in the story of the revelation of the glory of God.

In like manner, suppose for a moment that you were a distant cousin of Elimelech. You too have suffered under the drought in the Promised Land. Unlike your cousin, however, you have stayed in the land that God has given you. You attend to the sacrifices that God has established. God, in his mercy, helps you grasp that the blood of bulls and goats cannot atone for sin. You trust that one day he will send the seed of the woman to crush the head of the serpent. You trust that God will provide the perfect sacrifice, just as he did for your father Abraham. In short, you repent and believe that which has been revealed, and God accounts it to you as righteousness. You have been redeemed. Your name, life's work, and zeal have not been recorded in the great book of redemptive history, the Bible, but you are still on that stage on which God manifests his glory.

God created the universe so that he might manifest his glory. His glory is displayed not only in the efficiency of the universe, but in its beauty. But his glory is also the reason for all that happens within the universe. Central to that, of course, is God's work of redemption on behalf of the elect. Much of what this book has been about is the glory of God in the redemption of sinners. As I began this chapter, I suggested that a Reformed understanding of the redemption of sinners, and it alone, affords God the glory due his name. We who, by the grace of God alone, embrace the Reformed faith, alone can declare *soli Deo gloria*.

But God's pursuit of his glory was not finished when he rested on the seventh day. Creation wasn't the end of the story, but the beginning. In like manner, Jesus was not finished when he entered into his reward and sat at the right hand of the Father. While there is nothing more to the story than the glory of God, there is more to the story than creation and redemption. There is also the glorious story of the consummation of the kingdom of Jesus Christ.

History continues to move forward. And every step brings us closer and closer to that great climax of history. Scripture describes that climax in any number of ways. We are told in Daniel 2 that during the reign of Rome a stone, uncut by human hands, would come and destroy that kingdom. Greater still, that stone would become a great mountain and fill the whole earth. Scripture likewise tells us that the Son will sit at the right hand of the Father until all his enemies are destroyed. Scripture also tells us that a day is coming when every knee will bow and every tongue will confess that Jesus is Lord.

If we stop looking at the story once we have established that we have been redeemed, we fail to live in light of this Reformation principle of *soli Deo gloria*. If we think that the greatest thing about God is that he thinks we are great, we have made ourselves the end and God the means. We are upside-down idolaters. It is true and it is glorious that God loves us and has redeemed us. But he has done this, not because we are so worthy, but because he is so worthy. We have been redeemed for a purpose, that we might eternally inhabit the kingdom of Jesus Christ. And that has happened, not of or for ourselves, but of and for him who redeemed us. In the new heavens and the new earth, we will exist for the same purpose that we now exist, to show forth the glory of God. He is glorified in the remaking of all things, in the fulfillment by the Second Adam of the charge given to the first, to exercise dominion over the creation for the glory of God. That day is coming. Glory be to God alone.

History begins with glory, as God does the unfathomable, speaking the universe into existence. He shows forth his power in doing so. He shows forth his beauty in how he arranges his creation. He shows forth his love in establishing a garden for the man and the woman. And then comes the Fall, which, as with all things, redounds to the glory of God. He will show forth his just wrath on some of the fallen. With others he will manifest his great mercy. Even here he shows forth his glory in creating the beautiful gospel, which marries justice and mercy. His Son suffers for us the righteous wrath of the Father. In mercy we are passed over. Justice and mercy kiss, and we receive a great reward. We become not only the sons of God, but citizens of his kingdom. But it is not enough for us to be redeemed. God's first charge must still be met. Jesus came not just to redeem, but to walk out of the tomb as the firstborn of the new creation. He continues to exercise dominion over us, as he pulls the weeds from our hearts, and as we bear fruit for him.

History then will end with the Christ having conquered all his enemies, with all the creation being a garden, with those who are redeemed serving as faithful citizens of this consummated kingdom. In the meantime, however, we do not merely wait. Rather, being faithful to our call to seek the glory of God alone in all that we do, we make more and more manifest the reign of Jesus our King. As we show forth our own obedience to the king, our labors become less and less wheat and chaff, and what remains is strengthened.

This is why we take the time to honor the work of my father, Dr. R. C. Sproul. He has proved himself to be a faithful steward, busy about the Master's business. He has spoken the word of the Master, not just forcefully, but faithfully. He has learned to fear no man, and to fear God. He has proved not to be only a teacher of the Word of God, but also to be taught by it. He has followed in the path laid down before him. We pray that he will continue for many more years to fight the good fight, to finish the race, to keep the faith. And for that we give all glory, praise, and honor to God alone, just as he would want it.

NOTES

CHAPTER 1: TOTAL DEPRAVITY

1 Millard J. Erickson, *Concise Dictionary of Christian Theology* (Grand Rapids: Baker, 1986), 15.

2 John Calvin, *Institutes of the Christian Religion,* ed. John T. McNeill, trans. Ford Lewis Battles (Philadelphia: Westminster, 1960), 2.1.8.

3 The Confession of Faith, 6.4.

4 William Graham, *Lectures on Human Nature,* ed. Joseph Glass (1796), 75.

5 The Shorter Catechism, Q. 35.

6 Alasdair C. MacIntyre, *After Virtue: A Study in Moral Theory,* 2d. ed. (Notre Dame, Ind.: University of Notre Dame Press, 1984).

7 Calvin, *Institutes,* 4.1.20.

8 James Montgomery Boice, *Romans: An Expositional Commentary: The Reign of Grace* (Grand Rapids: Baker, 1992), 702.

CHAPTER 2: *SOLA SCRIPTURA*

1 The doctrine of justification by faith alone was the "material principle" of the Reformation.

2 For a more exhaustive examination of the doctrine of *sola Scriptura* in its historical context, see Keith A. Mathison, *The Shape of Sola Scriptura* (Moscow, Idaho: Canon Press, 2001).

3 Heiko Oberman, *The Dawn of the Reformation* (Edinburgh: T & T Clark, 1986), 280.

4 See, for example, Oberman, *Dawn of the Reformation,* 269–96; J. N. D. Kelly, *Early Christian Doctrines,* rev. ed. (San Francisco: Harper Collins, 1978), 29–51; R. P. C. Hanson, *Tradition in the Early Church* (London: SCM Press, 1962); F. F. Bruce, *Tradition: Old and New* (Grand Rapids: Zondervan, 1970).

5 For a summary of the evidence against the idea that Basil and Augustine taught Tradition II, see Mathison, *The Shape of Sola Scriptura,* 33–35, 39–42.

6 Ibid., 78–79.

7 Cited in Philip Schaff, *The Principle of Protestantism,* ed. Bard Thompson and George H. Bricker, Lancaster Series on the Mercersburg Theology, vol. 1 (Philadelphia: United Church Press, 1964), 117n.

8 Alister McGrath, *The Genesis of Doctrine: A Study in the Foundations of Doctrinal Criticism* (Oxford: Basil Blackwell, 1990), 118.

9 Oberman, *Dawn of the Reformation,* 289–90.

10 For more on this phenomenon, see Nathan O. Hatch, *The Democratization of American Christianity* (New Haven: Yale University Press, 1989); Nathan O. Hatch, "Sola Scriptura and Novus Ordo Seclorum," in *The Bible in America: Essays in Cultural History,* ed. Nathan O. Hatch and Mark A. Noll (New York: Oxford University Press, 1982).

11 Hatch, *Democratization of American Christianity,* 69.

12 Ibid., 81.

13 All of the following are cited in Hatch, *Democratization of American Christianity,* 179–82.

14 Samuel Miller, *The Utility and Importance of Creeds and Confessions* (Greenville, S.C.: A Press, 1991), 15.

15 For a good example of how liberals used the concept of Tradition 0 to infiltrate one denomination, see George Marsden, *Fundamentalism and American Culture* (New York: Oxford University Press, 1980), 171–72.

16 Two of the most obvious examples are the rejection of the traditional Christian doctrine of God by the open theists and the rejection of traditional Christian eschatology by the full preterists.

17 Different systematic theology texts use different terms to describe this attribute of Scripture (e.g., *perfection, completeness,* and *sufficiency*). The sufficiency of Scripture is discussed separately in order to avoid confusion.

18 Wayne Grudem, *Systematic Theology* (Grand Rapids: Zondervan, 1994), 127.

19 E.g., John F. MacArthur Jr., "The Sufficiency of the Written Word," in *Sola Scriptura: The Protestant Position on the Bible,* ed. Don Kistler (Morgan, Pa.: Soli Deo Gloria, 1995), 165.

20 E.g., John H. Gerstner, "Justification by *Faith* Alone: The Nature of Justifying Faith," in *Justification by Faith Alone,* ed. Don Kistler (Morgan, Pa.: Soli Deo Gloria, 1995), 113.

21 The statement "Scripture interprets Scripture" means that the meaning of individual passages of Scripture is illuminated and clarified by examining it in light of the remainder of Scripture. It does not mean that biblical interpretation can occur apart from the action of human agents.

22 Charles Hodge, *Systematic Theology* (Grand Rapids: Eerdmans, 1989), 1:154.

CHAPTER 3: UNCONDITIONAL ELECTION

1 John Calvin, *Sermons on the Epistle to the Ephesians,* trans. Arthur Golding, rev. ed. (Edinburgh: Banner of Truth Trust, 1973), 24.

2 Ibid., 42–43.

3 Ibid., 47.

CHAPTER 4: *SOLA FIDE*

1 John Calvin, *Institutes of the Christian Religion,* ed. John T. McNeill, trans. Ford Lewis Battles (Philadelphia: Westminster, 1960), 3.11.1.

2 Ibid., 3.11.19.

3 The Shorter Catechism (1647), Q. 33.

4 Cf. Daniel 9, in which, within a covenant context (9:4), the righteousness of God serves as the foundation for his judgment, but also as the ground on which an appeal for mercy is made.

5 In essence, Elijah's prayer that it would not rain was an expression of his conviction that God would keep his covenant promises and threats (e.g., Deut. 28:24), and it was a confident request that he do so.

6 This polemical context explains the way in which, in Book 3 of the *Institutes,* he expounds union with Christ and the Christian life before dealing with justification.

7 John Calvin, *The Epistles of Paul the Apostle to the Romans and the Thessalonians,* ed. D. W. and T. F. Torrance, trans. R. Mackenzie (Edinburgh: Oliver and Boyd, 1960), 167.

8 The Shorter Catechism, Q. 33.

9 Calvin, *Institutes,* 3.1.1

10 Ibid.

11 The Confession of Faith, 11.2.

12 The statements of the Council of Trent on justification exemplify this perspective. See Philip Schaff, *The Creeds of Christendom* (New York: Harper, 1877), 2:89–118.

13 This point has been made by theologians as diverse as Calvin (*Institutes,* 3.2.7) and Bultmann (in *Theological Dictionary of the New Testament,* ed. G. Kittel and G. Friedrich, trans. G. W. Bromiley, vol. 6 [Grand Rapids: Eerdmans, 1968], 227).

14 John Murray, *Collected Writings,* vol. 2, *Select Lectures in Systematic Theology* (Edinburgh: Banner of Truth Trust, 1977), 237.

15 The Heidelberg Catechism, Q. 21.

16 Calvin, *Institutes,* 3.2.7.

17 B. B. Warfield, *Biblical Doctrines* (New York: Oxford University Press, 1929), 504.

18 Since "this" (*touto*) is neuter, grammar alone cannot determine the antecedent to which reference is made—whether grace, faith, or salvation.

19 Otto Weber, *Foundations of Dogmatics,* trans. D. L. Guder (Grand Rapids: Eerdmans, 1981–83), 2:261.

20 Philip Edgcumbe Hughes, *Paul's Second Epistle to the Corinthians,* NICNT (Grand Rapids: Eerdmans, 1962), 182–83 (emphasis his).

21 John Murray, *Redemption—Accomplished and Applied* (Grand Rapids: Eerdmans, 1955), 131.

22 Calvin, *Institutes,* 3.2.20.

23 The Confession of Faith, 11.2.

CHAPTER 6: *SOLA GRATIA*

1 In Heiko A. Oberman, *Forerunners of the Reformation: The Shape of Late Medieval Thought,* trans. Paul L. Nyhus (Philadelphia: Fortress Press, 1981), 151–64.

2 Charles Finney, *The Memoirs of Charles G. Finney,* ed. Garth M. Rosell and Richard A. G. Dupuis (Grand Rapids: Zondervan, 1989), 23, 27.

3 Unless otherwise indicated, quotations of Finney are taken from Charles Finney, *Finney's Systematic Theology,* ed. J. H. Fairchild, abridged (Minneapolis: Bethany Fellowship, 1976).

4 Benjamin B. Warfield, *The Plan of Salvation,* rev. ed. (Grand Rapids: Eerdmans, 1975), 33.

5 See, e.g., Benjamin Breckinridge Warfield, *Perfectionism,* ed. Samuel G. Craig (Philadelphia: Presbyterian and Reformed, 1958).

6 Charles G. Finney, *Revivals of Religion* (Westwood, N.J.: Fleming H. Revell, n.d.), 4–5.

7 Ibid., 5.

8 H. Richard Niebuhr, *The Kingdom of God in America* (New York: Harper and Row, 1937), 2.

9 Harry Conn, foreword to Finney, *Finney's Systematic Theology,* vii.

10 Christopher Lasch, *The Culture of Narcissism: American Life in an Age of Diminishing Expectations* (New York: Warner Books, 1979), 22.

11 Ibid., 26.

12 Ibid., 33.

CHAPTER 8: *SOLUS CHRISTUS*

1 Tony Evans, *Totally Saved: Understanding, Experiencing and Enjoying the Greatness of Your Salvation* (Chicago: Moody Press, 2002), 355.

2 The eternal state of those who die as infants (or even as adults with severely limited intellectual capacity) is a separate question. The doctrine of infant salvation in no way lends support to the notion that non-Christian adults who have never received the gospel can be saved. I have dealt at length with this issue in two messages available

on tape from Grace to You (1-800-55-GRACE). The tapes are entitled "The Salvation of Babies Who Die" (parts 1 and 2), and the tape numbers are GC 80-242 and GC 80-243.

3 Evans, *Totally Saved,* 358.

4 Ibid., 361.

5 Ibid., 354.

6 Ibid., 365.

7 "Is 'Natural Theology' a Form of Deism?" Online: http://www.faithdefenders.com/sermons/pro7.html.

8 Raimundo Pannikar, *The Unknown Christ of Hinduism* (London: Darton, Longman and Todd, 1964), 54.

9 Peter Kreeft, *Ecumenical Jihad* (San Francisco: Ignatius, 1996), 31.

10 Evans, *Totally Saved,* 360.

CHAPTER 9: PERSEVERANCE OF THE SAINTS

1 All New Testament quotations are from the writer's translation found in *The Christian Counselor's New Testament* (Nutley, N.J.: Presbyterian and Reformed, 1977).

2 Foreordination itself settles the issue for any thinker. It would be a contradiction in terms for God to "foreordain" that which may not or will not come to pass.

3 This is an Arminian group, founded by Thomas and Alexander Campbell, that claims to be the only true church. Campbellites refuse to capitalize the word "churches" and claim not to be a denomination.

4 The verb *to apostatize* means "to stand off from."

5 Cf. Rev. 3:19.

6 I.e., the sanctification that is always present, giving evidence of the fact that one is saved.

CONTRIBUTORS

Jay E. Adams is former president of the National Association of Nouthetic Counselors and former director of advanced studies at Westminster Theological Seminary in California.

Edmund P. Clowney is teacher in residence at Trinity Presbyterian Church in Charlottesville, Virginia, and former president of Westminster Theological Seminary in Philadelphia.

Sinclair B. Ferguson is senior minister of St. George's Tron-Parish in Glasgow, Scotland, and former professor of theology at Westminster Theological Seminary in Philadelphia.

W. Robert Godfrey is president of and professor of church history at Westminster Theological Seminary in California.

Michael S. Horton is host of the "White Horse Inn" radio broadcast, editor-in-chief of *Modern Reformation* magazine, and associate professor of historical theology at Westminster Theological Seminary in California.

John F. MacArthur is pastor-teacher of Grace Community Church in Sun Valley, California, and president of The Master's College and Seminary.

Keith A. Mathison is director of curriculum development for Ligonier Ministries and assistant editor of *Tabletalk* magazine.

Martin Murphy is founding pastor of Wiregrass Presbyterian Church in Dothan, Alabama.

O. Palmer Robertson is principal and director of the African Bible College in Kampala, Uganda, and adjunct professor of Old Testament at Knox Theological Seminary in Fort Lauderdale, Florida.

R. C. Sproul Jr. is director of the Highlands Study Center, editor-in-chief of *Tabletalk* magazine, and associate pastor of teaching at Saint Peter Presbyterian Church in Bristol, Tennessee.

Douglas J. Wilson is pastor of Christ Church in Moscow, Idaho, and editor of *Credenda/Agenda* magazine.

INDEX OF SCRIPTURE

211

213